fast & simple Family Recipes

A J.B. Fairfax Press Publication

INTRODUCTION

Feed your family in a flash with this collection of simple but imaginative recipes specially created with the busy cook in mind. Here are recipes to see you through every occasion from mid-week meals to special events. Incorporating methods for both microwave and conventional cooking, these recipes will have you spending less time in the kitchen and more on the things that really matter – and enjoying good food is one of them . . .

EDITORIAL
Food Editor: Rachel Blackmore
Editors: Margaret Gore, Kirsten John, Linda Venturoni
Editorial and Production Assistant: Danielle Thiris
Editorial Coordinator: Margaret Kelly
UK Food Consultant: Katie Swallow

Photography: Phil Wymant
Styling: Susan Brazel
Cover Photography: Quentin Bacon
Cover Styling: Donna Hay

DESIGN AND PRODUCTION
Manager: Sheridan Carter
Layout and Design: Lulu Dougherty
Senior Production Editor: Anna Maguire
Production Editor: Sheridan Packer
Cover Design: Michele Withers

Published by J.B. Fairfax Press Pty Ltd
80-82 McLachlan Ave
Rushcutters Bay, NSW, 2011, Australia
A.C.N. 003 738 430

Formatted by J.B. Fairfax Press Pty Limited
Printed by Toppan Printing Co, Singapore
PRINTED IN SINGAPORE

The Custom Book Company is a joint venture of Century Magazines Pty Limited A.C.N. 003 400 904 and R.A. Ramsay Pty Limited A.C.N. 001 864 446

JBFP 372
Includes Index
1 86343 207 8

DISTRIBUTION AND SALES
United Kingdom: J.B. Fairfax Press Limited
Ph: (0933) 40 2330 Fax: (0933) 40 2234

ABOUT THIS BOOK

INGREDIENTS
Unless otherwise stated the following ingredients are used in this book:

Cream	Double, suitable for whipping
Flour	White flour, plain or standard
Sugar	White sugar

WHAT'S IN A TABLESPOON?
AUSTRALIA
1 tablespoon = 20 mL or 4 teaspoons
NEW ZEALAND
1 tablespoon = 15 mL or 3 teaspoons
UNITED KINGDOM
1 tablespoon = 15 mL or 3 teaspoons
The recipes in this book were tested in Australia where a 20 mL tablespoon is standard. The tablespoon in the New Zealand and the United Kingdom sets of measuring spoons is 15 mL. For recipes using baking powder, gelatine, bicarbonate of soda, small quantities of flour and cornflour, simply add another teaspoon for each tablespoon specified.

CANNED FOODS
Can sizes vary between countries and manufacturers. You may find the quantities in this book are slightly different to what is available. Purchase and use the can size nearest to the suggested size in the recipe.

MICROWAVE IT
Where microwave instructions occur in this book, a microwave oven with a 650 watt output has been used. Wattage on domestic microwave ovens varies between 500 and 700 watts, so it may be necessary to vary cooking times slightly depending on the wattage of your oven.

CONTENTS

SMART STARTERS

Delicious appetisers and first courses are important to the enjoyment of a meal as they stimulate the palate with tangy flavours and delightful textures. Try these quick and easy recipes; they are ideal for entertaining or for casual light snacks at family meals.

PATE BOUCHEES

Oven temperature
180°C, 350°F, Gas 4

For variety, choose a favourite meat, game or seafood pâté from the wide selection of prepared pâté products now available in delicatessens and speciality food stores.

250 g/8 oz cream cheese, softened
200 g/6$^{1}/_{2}$ oz prepared pâté
2 teaspoons chopped fresh parsley
24 x 4 cm/1$^{1}/_{2}$ in vol-au-vent cases
$^{1}/_{4}$ red pepper, cut into thin slivers

1 Place cream cheese, pâté and parsley in a food processor or blender and process until smooth.

2 Place vol-au-vent cases on a baking tray and bake for 10 minutes or until crisp. Spoon or pipe pâté mixture into each vol-au-vent case, top with a sliver of red pepper and serve immediately.

Makes 24

Pâté Bouchées

SATAY CHICKEN WINGS

Oven temperature
190°C, 375°F, Gas 5

1 kg/2 lb chicken wings

PEANUT MARINADE

$^1/_2$ cup/125 mL/4 fl oz coconut milk
$^1/_4$ cup/60 g/2 oz peanut butter
1 clove garlic, crushed
1 teaspoon sesame oil
$^1/_2$ teaspoon curry powder
$^1/_4$ teaspoon chilli powder
pinch cayenne pepper
pinch five spice powder

To microwave, complete steps 1 and 2 above. Place drained wings in a large, shallow microwavable dish and cook, uncovered on HIGH (100%) for 6 minutes. Turn wings over, cook for 5 minutes, brush with marinade and test for doneness, giving extra time if necessary.

1 Cut through chicken wings at each joint to make three pieces, discarding wing tips. (Chicken wing tips can be set aside to make stock and frozen for other uses.)

2 To make marinade, place coconut milk, peanut butter, garlic, sesame oil, curry powder, chilli powder, cayenne pepper and five spice powder in a bowl and mix to combine. Add chicken wing pieces and toss to coat. Cover and marinate in the refrigerator for 30 minutes or overnight.

3 Drain wings, reserving marinade. Place wings on a wire rack in a baking dish and bake for 15 minutes, turn chicken over, brush with reserved marinade and cook for 15 minutes longer or until golden and cooked through. Serve hot or cold.

Serves 4

FISH NUGGETS
Microwave

500 g/1 lb firm white fish fillets
1 cup/60 g/2 oz breadcrumbs, made from stale bread
1 onion, finely chopped
1 carrot, finely grated
1 egg, beaten
1 tablespoon mayonnaise
$^1/_2$ teaspoon dried dill
freshly ground black pepper
1 cup/45 g/1$^1/_2$ oz cornflakes, crushed

Serve these crispy nuggets hot with tartare sauce. To make a quick tartare sauce, fold 1-2 tablespoons each of finely chopped fresh parsley, sweet gherkin pickles, onion and capers into 1 cup/250 mL/8 fl oz prepared mayonnaise. Mix well and refrigerate until ready to serve.

1 Place fish in a shallow microwavable dish, cover and cook on HIGH (100 %) for 4 minutes. Set fish aside to cool, then chop finely.

2 Place fish, breadcrumbs, onion, carrot, egg, mayonnaise, dill and black pepper to taste in a bowl and mix to combine.

3 Shape tablespoons of mixture into ovals or nuggets and roll in cornflake crumbs to coat. Arrange half the nuggets in a large shallow microwavable dish. Cook on HIGH (100%) for 2 minutes, turn nuggets over and cook for 2 minutes longer or until cooked through. Repeat with remaining nuggets.

Serves 4

Satay-style Oysters

SATAY-STYLE OYSTERS

2 tablespoons smooth peanut butter
$^1/_3$ cup/90 g/3 oz sour cream
Tabasco sauce
12 fresh oysters, on the half shell
2 rashers bacon, chopped
chopped fresh parsley or coriander

1 Place peanut butter, sour cream and Tabasco sauce to taste in a bowl and mix to combine.

2 Place oysters in a baking tin, place a spoonful of mixture onto each oyster and sprinkle with bacon. Cook under a preheated hot grill for 2-3 minutes or until oysters are golden . Sprinkle with parsley or coriander and serve.

Serves 2

Serve as an entrée with a squeeze of fresh lemon or lime juice and buttered fresh brown bread.

FLAKY SALMON PARCELS

Oven temperature
200°C, 400°F, Gas 6

These parcels may be
prepared in advance,
wrapped and frozen for up
to 4 weeks before baking.
Thaw overnight in the
refrigerator and bake as
directed.

125 g/4 oz cottage cheese
125 g/4 oz canned salmon, drained
and flaked
1 egg, lightly beaten
1 spring onion, chopped
1 teaspoon lemon juice
$1/2$ teaspoon sugar
6 sheets filo pastry
melted butter

1 Place cottage cheese, salmon, egg,
spring onion, lemon juice and sugar in
a bowl and mix to combine.

2 Cut each sheet of pastry lengthwise
in half. Working with one pastry strip
at a time, brush with melted butter,
place a tablespoon of salmon mixture
at one end of the strip, fold pastry edges
over mixture, tuck in sides and roll up
like a Swiss roll to form a neat parcel.

3 Place parcels on a baking tray, brush
with melted butter and bake for
15 minutes or until pastry is golden.

Makes 12

HONEYED MEATBALLS

Left: Flaky Salmon Parcels
Below: Honeyed Meatballs

500 g/1 lb lean pork mince
500 g/1 lb chicken mince
1 cup/60 g/2 oz breadcrumbs, made
from stale bread
1 onion, finely chopped
2 cloves garlic, crushed
1 teaspoon finely grated fresh ginger
$^1/_2$ cup/170 g/5$^1/_2$ oz honey
$^1/_4$ cup/60 mL/2 fl oz soy sauce
1 tablespoon sherry
$^1/_2$ teaspoon chilli sauce
$^3/_4$ cup/140 g/4$^1/_2$ oz rice flour
1 cup/250 mL/8 fl oz vegetable oil
$^1/_2$ teaspoon sesame oil

1   Place pork, chicken, breadcrumbs, onion, garlic, ginger, honey, soy sauce, sherry and chilli sauce in a bowl and mix to combine. Roll tablespoons of mixture into balls and toss in rice flour to coat. Shake off excess.

2   Heat vegetable and sesame oils in a large saucepan until a cube of bread dropped in browns in 50 seconds and deep fry balls, a few at a time, for 5 minutes, or until golden brown. Drain on absorbent kitchen paper.

Makes 40

To make rice flour, process rice in a food processor or blender until fine. Rice flour gives the meatballs a crisp surface, however plain flour may be substituted.

PEPERONI PINWHEELS

Oven temperature
220°C, 425°F, Gas 7

100 g/3¹/₂ oz peperoni, finely chopped
1 onion, finely chopped
1 tablespoon chopped fresh parsley
¹/₄ teaspoon chilli powder
¹/₄ teaspoon dried oregano leaves
freshly ground black pepper
¹/₂ cup/60 g/2 oz grated Parmesan
cheese
500 g/1 lb prepared puff pastry
milk

1 Place peperoni, onion, parsley, chilli powder, oregano, black pepper to taste and half the Parmesan cheese in a bowl and mix well to combine.

2 Roll out half the pastry at a time on a lightly floured surface to a 23cm/9 in square. Spoon half the filling evenly over each pastry square, leaving a 2 cm/³/₄ in border. Brush pastry edges with milk. Fold in sides and roll up like a Swiss roll.

3 Using a sharp knife, cut each roll into 1 cm/¹/₂ in slices, place on lightly oiled baking trays and sprinkle with remaining Parmesan cheese.

4 Bake for 15-20 minutes or until pastry is puffed and golden brown. Serve hot or cold.

Makes 36

To freeze, prepare pinwheels to the end of step 3, freeze slices on the trays until firm, then pack into freezer bags, excluding all air. Label, date and freeze until needed. To serve, place pinwheels on baking tray and proceed with step 4.

BEAN DIP

315 g/10 oz canned butter or lima beans, drained and rinsed
1 tablespoon vegetable oil
1 tablespoon fruit chutney
1 clove garlic, crushed
2 tablespoons chopped fresh parsley
Tabasco sauce
freshly ground black pepper

Place beans, oil, chutney and garlic in a food processor or blender and process until smooth. Stir in parsley, Tabasco sauce and black pepper to taste and serve immediately with water biscuits or vegetable crudités.

Makes 1¹/₂ cups/375 g/12 oz

If using dried butter or lima beans, soak 155 g/5 oz overnight in water, drain and cook in a large saucepan of simmering water for 1¹/₂-2 hours or until very tender.

PINEAPPLE WITH TARRAGON CREAM

1 large ripe pineapple, skin removed
1¹/₂ tablespoons lemon juice
2 teaspoons sugar
chopped fresh tarragon or parsley

TARRAGON CREAM
2 egg yolks
¹/₄ cup/60 mL/2 fl oz tarragon vinegar
1 tablespoon sugar
freshly ground black pepper
²/₃ cup/170 mL/5¹/₂ fl oz cream
(double), whipped

To microwave tarragon cream, place egg yolks, vinegar, sugar and black pepper to taste in a microwavable bowl and whisk to combine. Cook on MEDIUM HIGH (70%) for 1¹/₂ minutes, stopping to whisk every 20 seconds. Set aside to cool slightly and fold whipped cream into mixture. If the cream is left out, tarragon cream may be made up to two weeks in advance and stored, covered, in the refrigerator. Fold in cream just before serving.

1 Cut pineapple into bite-sized chunks, place in a bowl, sprinkle with lemon juice and sugar and refrigerate until ready to serve.

2 To make Tarragon Cream, place egg yolks, vinegar, sugar and black pepper to taste in a heatproof bowl set over a saucepan of simmering water and heat, stirring constantly, until mixture thickens. Remove bowl from pan, set aside to cool slightly and fold whipped cream into mixture.

3 Arrange pineapple pieces on a serving platter accompanied by a bowl of tarragon cream garnished with chopped tarragon or parsley. Cooked prawns and melon balls are equally delicious dipped into tarragon cream.

Serves 6

WHISKY PATE

125 g/4 oz butter
1 kg/2 lb chicken livers, cleaned and roughly chopped
¹/₂ cup/125 mL/4 fl oz chicken stock
¹/₂ cup/75 g/2¹/₂ oz quick cooking oats
¹/₂ bunch fresh parsley, chopped
¹/₄ cup/60 mL/2 fl oz whisky
2 hard-boiled eggs, chopped
freshly ground black pepper

If desired for longer storage, spoon melted, clarified butter over the top of pâté to seal completely and refrigerate. Chopped fresh parsley and other herbs can be frozen in 1 tablespoon quantities for later use. If large quantities of parsley are on hand, chop, freeze in ice-cube trays, remove the cubes and store in plastic bags in the freezer until ready to use.

1 Melt butter in a saucepan over a medium heat, add chicken livers and cook, stirring, for 3 minutes or until livers are firm, but still pink in the centre. Stir stock and oats into pan, bring to simmering and simmer for 2 minutes longer. Remove pan from heat and allow mixture to cool slightly.

2 Place mixture in a food processor or blender, add parsley, whisky and eggs and process until smooth. Season to taste with black pepper.

3 Spoon mixture into individual pâté pots (or one large pâté terrine), cover and refrigerate for 24 hours. Serve with water crackers or Melba toast.

Serves 10

LIGHT MEALS

Light and delicious, these recipes are perfect for a starter at a dinner party or a relaxed weekend luncheon. Whatever the occasion, you can be sure that they'll look good and taste great.

MELON WITH BASIL DRESSING

½ rockmelon(cantaloupe), cut
into quarters
4 slices prosciutto or ham
4 large lettuce leaves of your choice
8 slices honeydew melon
8 slices watermelon
250 g/8 oz cherry tomatoes
fresh basil leaves

SWEET BASIL DRESSING
⅓ cup/90 mL/3 fl oz white vinegar
2 tablespoons chopped fresh basil
2 tablespoons vegetable oil
1 teaspoon brown sugar
freshly ground black pepper

1   To make dressing, place vinegar, chopped basil, oil, sugar and black pepper to taste in a screwtop jar and shake well to combine. Set aside to chill in the refrigerator.

2   Remove seeds from each rockmelon (cantaloupe) quarter. Cut flesh away from skin in one piece and cut crosswise into four segments. Replace melon segments on skin.

3   Roll up each slice of prosciutto or ham, cut into four and using a wooden toothpick or cocktail stick secure each roll to a melon segment.

4   Arrange each melon wedge on a lettuce leaf on a serving plate. Fan slices of honeydew melon and watermelon and place on either side of rockmelon (cantaloupe). Garnish with tomatoes and basil leaves. Drizzle dressing over melons and serve.

Serves 4

To take advantage of the season's fresh produce, any favourite combination of fresh fruits and sliced meat may be used as desired.

Melon with Basil Dressing

COUSCOUS TOMATOES

Oven temperature
200°C, 400°F, Gas 6

This dish can also be cooked in the microwave. Place oil, onion, red or green pepper and garlic in a microwavable dish and cook on HIGH (100%) for 1 minute, stir and cook for 1 minute longer. Stir stock, cumin, cayenne pepper and couscous into mixture, and cook for 1 minute, then continue from step 3. To cook filled tomatoes, place in a microwavable dish and cook on HIGH (100%) for 5 minutes.

6 medium tomatoes
fresh mint sprigs

MINTED COUSCOUS FILLING
1 tablespoon olive oil
1 onion, chopped
$^1/_2$ red or green pepper, chopped
1 clove garlic, crushed
$^3/_4$ cup/185 mL/6 fl oz hot chicken stock
$^1/_2$ teaspoon ground cumin
pinch cayenne pepper
$^1/_2$ cup/90 g/3 oz couscous
1 tablespoon chopped fresh mint
freshly ground black pepper

1   Slice tops off tomatoes, scoop out pulp from shells and reserve. Place shells, cut side down, on absorbent kitchen paper and set aside to drain.

2   To make filling, heat oil in a saucepan over a medium heat, add onion, red or green pepper and garlic and cook, stirring, for 3 minutes or until onion is golden. Add stock, cumin and cayenne pepper to pan and bring to the boil. Remove pan from heat, add couscous and chopped mint, mix well, cover and set aside for 15-20 minutes, or until couscous absorbs all the liquid.

3   Add $^1/_2$ cup/125 g/4 oz reserved tomato pulp and black pepper to taste to couscous mixture and toss to combine. Spoon mixture into tomato shells, place in a lightly greased baking dish and bake for 15 minutes or until golden and cooked. Garnish with mint sprigs and serve immediately.

Serves 6

CHAMPAGNE OYSTERS

Microwave

Toasted, chopped Brazil nuts, walnuts or pecans may be substituted for the macadamia nuts, if preferred.

24 fresh oysters on the half shell
1 cup/250 mL/8 fl oz champagne or dry sparkling wine
4 egg yolks
3 teaspoons lemon juice
125 g/4 oz butter, melted
1 tablespoon cream (double)
freshly ground black pepper
30 g/1 oz toasted macadamia nuts, chopped
snipped fresh chives

1   Remove oysters from shells and reserve shells. Place oysters and wine in a microwavable dish, cover and cook on MEDIUM (50%) for 2 minutes. Drain oysters and return to their shells.

2   Place egg yolks and lemon juice in a food processor or blender and process until smooth. With machine running, gradually add warm, melted butter and process until thick. Fold in cream and black pepper to taste.

3   Place a teaspoonful of sauce over each oyster, sprinkle with nuts and reheat oysters, 8 at a time, on MEDIUM (50%), for 20-25 seconds. Sprinkle with chives and serve.

Serves 4

SPICY SEAFOOD ENTREE

2 spring onions, sliced
1 clove garlic, crushed
2 tablespoons lemon juice
1 teaspoon finely grated fresh ginger
$^1/_4$ teaspoon chilli sauce
$^1/_2$ teaspoon ground turmeric
$^1/_2$ teaspoon ground cumin
$^1/_2$ teaspoon mustard seeds
$^1/_2$ teaspoon ground paprika
125 g/4 oz squid (calamari) tubes,
cleaned and sliced
125 g/4 oz uncooked prawns, shelled
and deveined
1 tablespoon vegetable oil

1   Place spring onions, garlic, lemon juice, ginger, chilli sauce, turmeric, cumin, mustard seeds and paprika in a large bowl and mix well to combine. Add squid (calamari) rings and prawns, toss to combine, cover and refrigerate overnight.

2   Heat oil in a frying pan over a medium heat, add squid (calamari), prawns and marinade, and cook, stirring constantly, for 3 minutes or until prawns just change colour. Serve immediately with rice.

Serves 2

Substitute 250 g/8 oz firm white fish fillets, cut into thin strips, instead of the squid (calamari) and prawns, if preferred.

EGGS FLORENTINE

45 g/1$^1/_2$ oz butter
1 bunch/500 g/1 lb English spinach,
shredded
1 teaspoon lemon juice
$^1/_4$ teaspoon ground nutmeg
freshly ground black pepper
1 tablespoon flour
$^3/_4$ cup/185 mL/6 fl oz milk
$^1/_2$ cup/60 g/2 oz grated tasty cheese
(mature Cheddar)
$^1/_4$ teaspoon prepared mustard
4 eggs, poached

1   Melt half the butter in a frying pan over a medium heat, add spinach and cook, stirring, for 3-5 minutes or until spinach wilts. Remove spinach from pan and drain well.

2   Place spinach, lemon juice, nutmeg and black pepper to taste in a bowl and mix well to combine. Spoon mixture into four individual shallow ramekins

or baking dishes and set aside to keep warm.

3   Melt remaining butter in a saucepan over a medium heat, add flour and cook, stirring, for 1 minute. Remove pan from heat and gradually whisk in milk. Return pan to heat and cook, stirring constantly, until sauce boils and thickens. Remove from heat, add half the tasty cheese (mature Cheddar), mustard and black pepper to taste and stir until cheese melts and mixture is smooth.

4   Spoon poached eggs onto spinach, drizzle sauce over eggs, sprinkle with remaining tasty cheese (mature Cheddar) and cook under a preheated hot grill for 3-5 minutes, or until cheese is bubbling. Serve immediately.

Serves 4

To save time, eggs may be poached ahead of time, placed into a bowl, covered with water and refrigerated until ready to use.

CORN AND KIBBLE QUICHE

Oven temperature
180°C, 350°F, Gas 4

10 slices multigrain bread, crusts
removed
75 g/2 1/2 oz butter, melted
1 onion, finely chopped
125 g/4 oz button mushrooms, sliced
freshly ground black pepper
4 eggs, beaten
3/4 cup/185 mL/6 fl oz cream (double)
315 g/10 oz canned corn kernels,
drained

Any leftover cooked
vegetables may be used
instead of the mushrooms
for an economical family-
style luncheon dish.

1   Use 1 tablespoon of melted butter to
brush over both sides of bread slices.
Line a 23 cm/9 in pie plate or quiche
tin with bread, pressing firmly to the
edges. Bake for 10 minutes or until set
and pale golden, remove and set aside
to cool.

2   Heat remaining butter in a frying
pan over a medium heat, add onion
and mushrooms and cook, stirring, for
2-3 minutes or until onion is just
coloured. Remove pan from heat,
season with black pepper to taste and
set aside to cool slightly.

3   Place eggs, cream and corn in a
bowl and mix to combine. Add
mushroom mixture, mix well and pour
into prepared bread case. Bake for
30-40 minutes or until filling is set.
Serve hot or cold with a crisp, green
salad.

Serves 4-6

VEGETABLE PIES

Oven temperature
200°C, 400°F, Gas 6

375 g/12 oz prepared puff pastry
1 tablespoon milk

VEGETABLE FILLING
1 tablespoon vegetable oil
2 rashers bacon, chopped
1 cup/90 g/3 oz finely shredded
cabbage
1 spring onion, chopped
1 carrot, finely grated
140 g/4 1/2 oz canned corn kernels,
drained
60 g/2 oz grated tasty cheese
(mature Cheddar)
milk

Cut the four pastry rounds
from four ready-rolled puff
pastry sheets. To avoid
waste, two smaller rounds
can be cut from each
sheet, making eight rounds.
Serve two per person.

1   Roll out pastry to a 34cm/13 1/2 in
square and cut into four 15 cm/6 in
circles and set aside.

2   To make filling, heat oil in a large
frying pan over a medium heat, add
bacon, cabbage and spring onion and
cook, stirring, for 3-4 minutes or until
cabbage just begins to wilt. Remove
pan from heat and set aside to cool
slightly. Stir carrot, corn and tasty
cheese (mature Cheddar)into cooled
mixture.

3   Place spoonfuls of filling in the
centre of each pastry round, brush the
edges with milk, then fold over to form
a half circle. Seal edges and, using a
fork, make a decorative pattern. Place
pies on a greased baking tray, brush
with milk, slit tops and bake for 15-20
minutes or until golden brown and
cooked through. Serve hot or cold.

Serves 4

Cucumber Boats

CUCUMBER BOATS

500 g/1 lb cooked prawns, shelled and
deveined
2 red apples, cored and chopped
$^1/_3$ cup/90 mL/3 fl oz lemon juice
2 tablespoons honey
2 teaspoons dried dill
1 stalk celery, chopped
45 g/1$^1/_2$ oz chopped walnuts
4 thin cucumbers
1 tablespoon French dressing
freshly ground black pepper
fresh dill sprigs (optional)

1   Place prawns, apples, lemon juice,
honey and dill in a bowl and toss to
combine. Cover and refrigerate for
1 hour. Add celery and walnuts to
mixture, toss to combine and set aside.

2   Slice cucumbers in half lengthwise,
scoop out seeds and discard. Sprinkle
cucumbers with dressing and black
pepper to taste. Fill each cucumber boat
with prawn mixture and garnish with
dill (if using).

Serves 8

To substitute dried herbs for
fresh, allow $^1/_4$ teaspoon
dried herbs for 1 teaspoon
fresh herbs.

CHEESY SPINACH SOUP
Microwave

15 g/¹/₂ oz butter
1 onion, finely chopped
1 clove garlic, crushed
¹/₄ teaspoon ground nutmeg
freshly ground black pepper
3 cups/750 mL/1¹/₄ pt chicken stock
500 g/1 lb frozen spinach, thawed,
reserve any liquid
60 g/2 oz grated tasty cheese (mature
Cheddar)
¹/₄ cup/60 g/2 oz sour cream

1 Place butter, onion, garlic, nutmeg and black pepper to taste in a microwavable dish and cook on HIGH (100%) for 2 minutes.

2 Place onion mixture, chicken stock, spinach and reserved liquid in a food processor or blender and process until smooth. Return soup to microwavable dish and cook on HIGH (100%) for 3 minutes longer.

3 Add cheese to soup, and stir until cheese melts. Ladle soup into individual serving bowls and stir sour cream into each to give a swirl effect.

Serves 6

For those who like strong cheese, Stilton may be used in place of the tasty cheese (mature Cheddar).

CURRIED CUCUMBER SOUP

30 g/1 oz butter
2 cucumbers, peeled, seeded and sliced
1 onion, chopped
¹/₂ teaspoon curry powder
pinch ground nutmeg
freshly ground black pepper
3 chicken stock cubes
2¹/₂ cups/600 mL/1 pt water
220 g/7 oz canned reduced-fat cream

1 Melt butter in a saucepan over a medium heat, add cucumbers, onion, curry powder, nutmeg and black pepper to taste and cook, stirring, for 5-7 minutes or until cucumbers are golden. Stir stock cubes and water into pan and bring to the boil. Reduce heat and simmer for 10-15 minutes or until cucumber is very tender. Remove pan from heat and set aside to cool slightly.

2 Place cucumber mixture in a food processor or blender and process until smooth. Add cream, mix well, cover and refrigerate until soup is very cold. Serve garnished with extra cucumber slices if desired.

Serves 4

This refreshing soup makes a delicious first course for a meal that features salad or quiche.

Curried Cucumber Soup

CHICKEN AND MUSHROOM PASTA
Microwave

375 g/12 oz fresh pasta

CHICKEN AND MUSHROOM
SAUCE
1 tablespoon cornflour
1¼ cups/315 mL/10 fl oz cream
(double)
2 tablespoons grated Parmesan cheese
1 tablespoon snipped fresh chives
375 g/12 oz button mushrooms,
halved
1 cup/125 g/4 oz cooked chicken
2 tablespoons Marsala or sherry
1 tablespoon chopped fresh parsley or
snipped fresh chives

1 Cook pasta in boiling water in a large saucepan following packet directions. Drain, set aside and keep warm.

2 To make sauce, place cornflour and cream in a microwavable bowl and blend until smooth. Stir in Parmesan cheese, chives, mushrooms, chicken and Marsala or sherry. Cook on HIGH (100%) for 10 minutes, stirring occasionally.

3 Pour mushroom mixture over pasta, sprinkle with parsley or chives and serve.

Serves 4

Take advantage of the range of fresh pastas available and choose one based on spinach, tomato or even pumpkin for interest and variety.

PASTA WITH SMOKED SALMON SAUCE
Microwave

375 g/12 oz fresh fettuccine

SMOKED SALMON SAUCE
45 g/1½ oz butter
1 clove garlic, crushed
4 spring onions, chopped
1 zucchini (courgette), cut into
julienne strips
125 g/4 oz button mushrooms, sliced
1 cup/250 mL/8 fl oz chicken stock
¾ cup/185 mL/6 fl oz cream (double)
3 teaspoons cornflour blended with
¼ cup/60 mL/2 fl oz white wine
2 tablespoons chopped fresh parsley
1 tablespoon tomato paste (pureé)
100 g/3½ oz smoked salmon, cut
into strips
2 tablespoons snipped fresh chives

1 Cook pasta in boiling water in a large saucepan following packet directions. Drain, set aside and keep warm.

2 To make sauce, place butter in a microwavable dish and melt on HIGH (100%) for 30 seconds. Add garlic, spring onions, zucchini (courgette) and mushrooms and cook for 5 minutes longer. Add stock, cream, blended cornflour and wine, parsley, tomato paste (pureé) and salmon, cook on HIGH (100%) until boiling, stir and cook for 2 minutes longer.

3 Toss sauce through cooked pasta, and garnish with snipped chives. Serve immediately.

Serves 4

A teaspoon of oil in the water will help prevent pasta from sticking together as it cooks.

PASTA WITH PESTO SAUCE

375 g/12 oz fresh pasta

PESTO SAUCE
2 bunches fresh basil leaves
3 cloves garlic, crushed
45 g/1^1/2 oz pine nuts, toasted
2 tablespoons olive oil
1 tablespoon lemon juice
freshly ground black pepper
freshly grated Parmesan cheese

1 Cook pasta in boiling water in a large saucepan following packet directions. Drain, set aside and keep warm.

2 To make sauce, place basil, garlic, pine nuts, olive oil, lemon juice and black pepper to taste in a food processor or blender and process until smooth.

3 Place pasta in a bowl, add sauce and toss lightly until well coated. Sprinkle with Parmesan cheese and serve.

Serves 4

To preserve a bumper crop of fresh basil, be sure to make large batches of Pesto Sauce and refrigerate in covered jars for use throughout the winter months.

SEAFOOD SAVOURY MUSHROOMS

12 open cup mushrooms
60 g/2 oz butter, melted
1 onion, chopped
1 clove garlic, crushed
1 tomato, peeled and chopped
2 tablespoons sherry
185 g/6 oz canned crab meat, drained and flaked
^{3}/4 cup/45 g/1^1/2 oz breadcrumbs, made from stale bread
freshly ground black pepper
30 g/1 oz grated tasty cheese (mature Cheddar)

1 Remove and chop mushroom stalks. Brush mushroom cups with a little of the butter, place on a lightly greased baking tray and set aside until required.

2 Heat remaining butter in a frying pan over a medium heat, add mushroom stalks, onion and garlic and cook, stirring, for 2-3 minutes or until onion is tender. Add tomato and sherry to pan and cook for 2-3 minutes or until liquid almost evaporates. Remove pan from heat, stir crab meat and ^{1}/2 cup/30 g/1 oz breadcrumbs into mixture and season with black pepper.

3 Spoon crab mixture into mushroom cups. Place remaining breadcrumbs and tasty cheese (mature Cheddar) in a bowl, mix to combine and sprinkle over crab mixture. Bake for 15 minutes or until mushrooms are tender.

Serves 4

Seafood Savoury Mushrooms

Oven temperature
200°C, 400°F, Gas 6

Canned red salmon, tuna or prawns are all suitable substitutes for the crab meat in this recipe.

LAMB PASTITSIO

1 tablespoon vegetable oil
1 onion, chopped
500 g/1lb minced lamb
200 g/6$^{1}/_{2}$ oz button mushrooms,
sliced
315 g/10 oz canned tomatoes,
undrained and mashed
1 teaspoon Worcestershire sauce
freshly ground black pepper
125 g/4 oz cream cheese, softened
$^{1}/_{2}$ cup/125 g/4 oz sour cream
1 teaspoon dried basil leaves
220 g/7 oz macaroni, cooked
60 g/2 oz grated tasty cheese
(mature Cheddar)

Accompany this simple meal with a salad made of your favourite vegetables. You might like to try a salad of raw spinach, orange segments, thinly sliced mushrooms and spring onions, tossed in a light vinaigrette dressing.

1   Heat oil in a large saucepan over a medium heat, add onion and cook, stirring, for 3 minutes or until onion is golden. Add lamb and cook for 5 minutes or until lamb is cooked through. Add mushrooms, tomatoes, Worcestershire sauce and black pepper to taste to pan and cook, stirring, for 5 minutes longer.

2   Place cream cheese, sour cream and basil in a bowl and mix to combine.

3   Spoon half the drained macaroni into a greased 8 cup/2 litre/3$^{1}/_{2}$ pt capacity ovenproof dish. Top with lamb mixture, then remaining macaroni. Spoon cream cheese mixture over top and sprinkle with tasty cheese (mature Cheddar). Bake for 20-25 minutes or until golden.

Serves 6

SCALLOPS IN PERNOD SAUCE

90 g/3 oz butter
4 spring onions, chopped
125 g/4 oz button mushrooms, sliced
750 g/1$^{1}/_{2}$ lb scallops, rinsed and
drained
2 tablespoons Pernod
2 tablespoons flour
1 cup/250 mL/8 fl oz milk
1 tablespoon lemon juice
2 egg yolks, beaten
freshly ground black pepper
$^{1}/_{2}$ cup/125 mL/4 fl oz cream
(double), lightly whipped
2 tablespoons flaked almonds, toasted
2 tablespoons chopped fresh parsley

This dinner party first course will look more substantial if served in crisp, hot vol-au-vent cases or over rice or toast.

1   Melt 45 g/1$^{1}/_{2}$ oz butter in a frying pan over a medium heat, add spring onions and mushrooms and cook, stirring, for 2 minutes. Add scallops and cook, stirring, for 1 minute.

2   Add Pernod, heat until fumes appear, then ignite with a lighted taper and toss scallops lightly in liquid until flames subside. Remove scallop mixture from pan, drain, reserve liquid and set aside.

3   Melt remaining butter in pan over a medium heat, add flour and cook, stirring, for 1 minute. Remove pan from heat and gradually whisk in milk. Return pan to heat and cook, stirring, until sauce boils and thickens.

4   Stir lemon juice, then egg yolks, black pepper to taste and reserved scallop liquid into mixture and simmer for 2 minutes. Fold in cream and scallop mixture, sprinkle with almonds and parsley and serve immediately.

Serves 6

VEGETABLE MAGIC

Give vegetables and salads new meaning with these versatile and satisfying dishes. Used as an accompaniment or as a main meal, you'll find them full of flavour and goodness.

SUNSHINE SLAW

1 pineapple
1/4 cup/60 mL/2 fl oz mayonnaise
1 tablespoon mango chutney
375 g/12 oz cabbage, shredded
1 tablespoon chopped fresh parsley
1 avocado, peeled and chopped
90 g/3 oz macadamia nuts, chopped

1 Halve pineapple lengthwise, remove flesh, chop and drain. Reserve pineapple shells.

2 Place mayonnaise and chutney in a large bowl and mix to combine. Add pineapple flesh, cabbage and parsley and toss well to combine. Cover and chill until needed.

3 Just prior to serving, add avocado to cabbage mixture, spoon into pineapple shells and sprinkle with macadamia nuts.

Serves 8

Shredded red cabbage, thin slivers of unpeeled red apple or diced fresh mango and grated carrot may all be added to this slaw for taste and variety.

Sunshine Slaw

ASPARAGUS WITH PECAN BEARNAISE

500 g/1 lb asparagus, trimmed

PECAN BEARNAISE
1/2 cup/125 mL/4 fl oz white wine
1/3 cup/90 mL/3 fl oz white vinegar
3 spring onions, halved lengthwise
2 egg yolks
250 g/8 oz butter, melted
60 g/2 oz pecans, chopped
2 tablespoons chopped spring onions
1 tablespoon chopped fresh parsley
1 teaspoon chopped fresh thyme or
1/2 teaspoon dried thyme

1 Boil, steam or microwave asparagus until just tender. Drain and rinse under cold running water to stop the cooking process, then drain well and chill.

2 To make béarnaise, heat wine, vinegar and halved spring onions in a saucepan over a medium heat until mixture begins to boil. Reduce heat and simmer until mixture reduces to yield 1/4 cup/60 mL/2 fl oz liquid. Strain and set aside to cool slightly.

3 Place egg yolks and reduced liquid into food processor or blender and process until combined. With machine running, gradually add warm, melted butter and process until thick. Fold in pecans, chopped spring onions, parsley and thyme.

4 To serve, place asparagus onto individual serving plates and drizzle with béarnaise.

This fresh springtime entrée looks pretty served with cornmeal muffins.

Serves 6

CELERY AND ALMOND SAUTE

45 g/1 1/2 oz butter
60 g/2 oz slivered almonds
3 rashers bacon, chopped
1 clove garlic, crushed
6 spring onions, chopped
8-10 stalks celery, diagonally sliced
1/3 cup/90 mL/3 fl oz dry white wine
freshly ground black pepper
2 tablespoons chopped fresh parsley

1 Melt half the butter in a frying pan over a medium heat, add almonds and cook, stirring, for 3 minutes or until golden brown. Remove almonds from pan and set aside. Add bacon to pan and cook, stirring, for 3-4 minutes or until crisp. Remove bacon from pan and set aside to drain on absorbent kitchen paper.

2 Melt remaining butter in the same pan, add garlic, spring onions and celery and cook, stirring, for 5 minutes or until celery is just tender.

3 Stir wine into mixture, cover and cook for 2 minutes longer. Season to taste with black pepper. Sprinkle with almonds, bacon and parsley and serve.

Crisp-cooked celery, toasted almonds and crisp bacon combine for a palate-pleasing 'crunch'.

Serves 6

SALAD DELMONICO

500 g/1lb cauliflower, cut into florets
½ cucumber, chopped
2 tomatoes, chopped
75 g/2½ oz stuffed olives
crisp lettuce cups

DELMONICO DRESSING
1¼ cups/315 g/10 oz sour cream
½ cup/125 mL/4 fl oz mayonnaise
60 g/2 oz blue vein cheese, grated
or crumbled
1 tablespoon white wine vinegar
1 tablespoon French mustard
Tabasco sauce
pinch cayenne pepper

1   To make dressing, place sour cream, mayonnaise, cheese, vinegar, mustard and Tabasco sauce and cayenne pepper to taste in a bowl and mix well to combine. Cover and chill until needed.

2   Boil, steam or microwave cauliflower until just tender. Drain and rinse under cold running water to stop the cooking process, then drain well and chill.

3   Place cauliflower, cucumber, tomatoes and olives in a bowl and toss to combine. Just prior to serving, spoon mixture into lettuce cups and drizzle with dressing.

This entrée or side salad can be converted to a protein-rich main course by the addition of slivered smoked ham or chicken, hard-boiled egg quarters or cubed Swiss or Gruyère cheese.

Salad Delmonico

Serves 6

Vegetables with Pecans

15 g/$\frac{1}{2}$ oz butter
6 spring onions, cut into
2.5 cm/1 in pieces
250 g/8 oz snow peas (mangetout)
125 g/4 oz button mushrooms, sliced
45 g/1$\frac{1}{2}$ oz pecan halves

Melt butter in a frying pan over a medium heat, add spring onions, snow peas (mangetout), mushrooms and pecans and cook, stirring, for 2 minutes or until snow peas (mangetout) are just tender. Serve immediately as a vegetable accompaniment.

Serves 6

Green beans, sliced diagonally may be substituted for snow peas (mangetout) and cashew nuts for the pecans.

Mushroom Vinaigrette Salad
Microwave

$\frac{1}{3}$ cup/90 mL/3 fl oz red wine vinegar
$\frac{1}{3}$ cup/90 mL/3 fl oz vegetable oil
1 onion, sliced
1 tablespoon chopped fresh parsley
1 tablespoon brown sugar
$\frac{1}{4}$ teaspoon mustard seeds
1 bay leaf
freshly ground black pepper
500 g/1 lb button mushrooms
cherry tomatoes
fresh parsley sprigs

1 Place vinegar, oil, onion, chopped parsley, sugar, mustard seeds, bay leaf and black pepper to taste in a microwavable dish, bring to the boil on HIGH (100 %) and cook for 1 minute. Add mushrooms to mixture, cover and cook for 1 minute longer. Set aside to cool slightly, then cover and chill until needed.

2 To serve, drain mushrooms and garnish with cherry tomatoes and parsley sprigs.

Serves 6

Prepare marinated mushrooms at least 24 hours ahead to give flavours time to mellow before serving.

Vegetables with Pecans

GREEN BEAN AND SPROUT TOSS

Use a variety of fresh bean and snow pea sprouts with alfalfa sprouts and even fresh watercress for colour, texture and delicious flavour.

15 g/¹/₂ oz butter
3 stalks celery, sliced
375 g/12 oz frozen, sliced green beans,
rinsed and drained
45 g/1¹/₂ oz bean sprouts
¹/₃ cup/90 mL/3 fl oz chicken stock
1 teaspoon dried dill
freshly ground black pepper

Melt butter in a frying pan or wok over a high heat, add celery and stir-fry for 1 minute. Add beans, bean sprouts, stock, dill and black pepper to taste and cook, stirring constantly, for 3 minutes longer or until heated through. Serve immediately.

Serves 4

GOLDEN CARROTS JULIENNE
Microwave

If preferred, use a combination of julienne strips of carrot, parsnip and beetroot to provide a colourful contrast to the zesty, horseradish sauce.

500 g/1 lb carrots, cut into thin strips
1¹/₂ tablespoons white wine
1 tablespoon grated onion
1¹/₂ tablespoons chopped fresh parsley
1 tablespoon mayonnaise
2 teaspoons horseradish cream
¹/₂ cup/30 g/1 oz breadcrumbs, made
from stale bread
15 g/¹/₂ oz butter, melted

1 Place carrots, wine and onion in a microwavable dish. Cover and cook on HIGH (100%) for 6 minutes or until tender. Drain.

2 Place parsley, mayonnaise and horseradish cream in a large bowl and mix to combine. Add carrots, toss to combine and transfer to a serving dish.

3 Place breadcrumbs and butter in a microwavable dish and cook on HIGH (100%) for 1 minute, stir and cook for 1 minute longer. Sprinkle breadcrumbs over carrots and serve.

Serves 6

SPICED RED CABBAGE

Microwave

Spiced Red Cabbage

¹/₂ red cabbage, finely shredded
1 green apple, grated
1 onion, chopped
¹/₃ cup/90 mL/3 fl oz dry red wine
2 tablespoons tarragon vinegar
15 g/¹/₂ oz butter
1 tablespoon brown sugar
freshly ground black pepper

Place cabbage, apple, onion, wine, vinegar, butter, sugar and black pepper to taste in a microwavable dish, stir to combine, cover and cook on HIGH (100%) for 8-10 minutes, stirring twice during cooking. Drain and serve as a vegetable accompaniment.

Serves 6

A generous splash of balsamic vinegar may be used in place of the tarragon vinegar, if preferred.

Avocado Salad

1 cos lettuce, torn into bite-size pieces
3 spring onions, diagonally sliced
1 carrot, cut into thin strips
30 g/1 oz pine nuts, toasted
1 teaspoon poppy seeds
1 avocado, stoned, peeled and sliced
2 teaspoons lemon juice
PIQUANT DRESSING
1¹/2 tablespoons olive oil
1 tablespoon red wine vinegar
1 teaspoon soy sauce
1/2 teaspoon sesame oil
1/2 teaspoon horseradish cream

1 Place lettuce, spring onions, carrot, pine nuts and poppy seeds into a serving bowl and toss to combine. Toss avocado slices with lemon juice and scatter over salad.

2 To make dressing, place olive oil, vinegar, soy sauce, sesame oil and horseradish cream in a screwtop jar and shake well to combine. Just prior to serving, drizzle dressing over salad.

Serves 6

Sliced fresh mango or segments of orange may be added to this attractive first course salad.

Fresh Tomato Salad

4 large tomatoes, sliced
1 white onion, very thinly sliced
4 tablespoons chopped fresh parsley
BASIL DRESSING
1/2 cup/125 mL/4 fl oz grape seed oil
1/4 cup/60 mL/2 fl oz white wine vinegar
1 clove garlic, crushed
2 teaspoons chopped fresh basil
1 teaspoon sugar
1/4 teaspoon dry mustard
freshly ground black pepper

1 To make dressing, place oil, vinegar, garlic, basil, sugar, dry mustard and black pepper to taste in a screwtop jar and shake well to combine.

2 Layer half the tomatoes, onion and parsley in a serving bowl, drizzle with half the dressing and repeat layers, using remaining ingredients. Cover and refrigerate until served.

Serves 8

Fresh coriander makes a most suitable alternative to basil when available.

Fresh Tomato Salad, Avocado Salad

BROC-CAULI WITH SOUR CREAM

Microwave

1 small cauliflower, cut into florets
500 g/1 lb broccoli, cut into florets
1¼ cups/315 g/10 oz sour cream
freshly ground black pepper
1 rasher bacon, chopped

1   Place cauliflower in a microwavable dish, cover and cook on HIGH (100%) for 5 minutes. Add broccoli to dish, cover and cook for 3-4 minutes longer. Drain vegetables, return to dish, set aside and keep warm.

2   Place sour cream and black pepper to taste in a small microwavable bowl and cook on HIGH (100%) for 30 seconds. Drizzle sour cream over cauliflower and broccoli.

3   Place bacon between two layers of absorbent kitchen paper in a microwavable dish and cook on HIGH (100%) for 1 minute. Sprinkle bacon across the top of cauliflower and broccoli, reheat for 1-2 minutes and serve immediately.

Serves 6

To cook these vegetables conventionally, steam the florets over simmering water in a covered saucepan until tender, drain well and arrange in a serving dish. Heat sour cream mixture in a small saucepan and crisp-fry bacon in a preheated medium grill.

BRUSSELS SPROUTS WITH APPLE

½ cup/125 mL/4 fl oz cold chicken stock
2 teaspoons cornflour
1 teaspoon vegetable oil
500 g/1 lb Brussels sprouts, halved
1 green apple, sliced
1 teaspoon dried basil leaves
freshly ground black pepper

1   Place stock, cornflour and oil in a saucepan, stir to blend then cook over a medium heat, stirring constantly, until sauce boils and thickens.

2   Fold Brussels sprouts into mixture, reduce heat, cover and simmer for 5 minutes. Stir apple into mixture and simmer, stirring occasionally, for 5 minutes longer, or until Brussels sprouts are just tender. Add basil and black pepper to taste, toss lightly and serve immediately.

Serves 4

This dish makes a delicious accompaniment for a roast pork or beef main course.

Mustard-glazed Vegetables

MUSTARD-GLAZED VEGETABLES

Microwave

12 baby new potatoes, halved
500 g/1 lb yellow squash, halved or
zucchini (courgettes), cut into chunks
500 g/1 lb Brussels sprouts, halved
1/2 cup/125 mL/4 fl oz apple juice
1 tablespoon wholegrain mustard

1   Place potatoes in a large microwavable dish, lightly sprinkle with water, cover and cook on HIGH (100%) for 6 minutes or until potatoes are tender. Remove to a plate and set aside to keep warm. Cook squash or zucchini (courgettes), then Brussels sprouts separately as directed for potatoes.

2   Return all vegetables to dish, fold in combined apple juice and mustard, cover and cook on HIGH (100%) for 2 minutes longer or until heated through. Toss lightly and serve immediately.

Serves 6

When Brussels sprouts are unavailable, use fresh asparagus or green beans, cut into short pieces, instead.

VEGETABLE RISOTTO

15 g/¹/₂ oz butter
1 onion, chopped
1 clove garlic, crushed
250 g/8 oz carrots, finely diced
1¹/₂ cups/330 g/10¹/₂ oz short grain
rice, washed
170 g/5¹/₂ oz zucchini (courgettes),
sliced
¹/₂ red or green pepper, sliced
2 cups/500 mL/16 fl oz tomato juice
1 cup/250 mL/8 fl oz vegetable or
chicken stock

1 Melt butter in a large saucepan over a medium heat, add onion, garlic and carrots and cook, stirring, for 3 minutes or until onion is tender. Add rice, zucchini (courgettes) and red or green pepper, and cook, stirring, for 2 minutes longer.

2 Stir tomato juice and stock into mixture and bring to the boil. Reduce heat, cover and simmer for 15-20 minutes or until rice is tender and liquid is absorbed.

Serves 6-8

Serve risotto with meat, fish or poultry or for a light vegetarian-style luncheon dish, sprinkle servings with toasted pine nuts or sesame seeds and perhaps a little grated tasty cheese (mature Cheddar).

GINGERED PUMPKIN

30 g/1 oz butter
2 teaspoons ground ginger
750 g/1¹/₂ lb pumpkin, cut into
serving-size pieces
¹/₃ cup/125 g/4 oz honey

Melt butter in a flameproof baking dish over a medium heat, add ginger and pumpkin and toss to coat evenly. Bake for 20 minutes, remove from oven, brush honey over pumpkin pieces, return to oven and cook for 20 minutes longer or until pumpkin is tender.

Serves 6

Oven temperature
200°C, 400°F, Gas 6

When pumpkin is unavailable, fresh carrots make a most suitable alternative.

Vegetable Risotto

BACON AND CHEESE-FILLED POTATOES

Microwave

4 potatoes, skin pierced
2 rashers bacon, chopped
1 onion, finely chopped
2 tablespoons sour cream
60 g/2 oz grated tasty cheese
(mature Cheddar)
freshly ground black pepper
pinch ground paprika

1   Place potatoes in a microwavable dish and cook on HIGH (100%) for 10 minutes or until cooked. Set aside to cool.

2   Place bacon and onion in a microwavable dish and cook on HIGH (100%) for 3 minutes or until onion is soft, drain and set aside.

3   Slice tops off potatoes, scoop out centres, leaving 1 cm/^{1}/$_2$ in shells. Place potato pulp in a bowl and mash. Add bacon, onion, sour cream, 45 g/1^1/$_2$ oz cheese and black pepper to taste and mix to combine.

4   Fill potato shells with bacon mixture, sprinkle with remaining cheese and paprika and heat on HIGH (100%) for 2 minutes or until cheese melts. Serve immediately.

Serves 4

Use care when scooping out the potato centres so that the skins remain intact and hold the filling properly.

POTATO AND AVOCADO BAKE

1 kg/2 lb baby new potatoes
1 avocado, stoned, peeled and roughly chopped
4 tablespoons chopped fresh parsley
3 tablespoons chopped fresh mint
3 tablespoons chopped fresh chives
2 teaspoons pink peppercorns
^{1}/$_4$ cup/60 g/2 oz sour cream
2 tablespoons Italian dressing
freshly ground black pepper

1   Boil, steam or microwave potatoes until just tender and place into an ovenproof dish.

2   Place avocado, parsley, mint, chives, pink peppercorns, sour cream, dressing and black pepper to taste in a bowl and lightly mix to combine. Fold mixture through potatoes, cover and bake for 15 minutes or until heated through.

Serves 8

Oven temperature
200°C, 400°F, Gas 6

This creamy herbed potato dish is delicious served hot with barbecued or cold meats.

44

MUSTARD AND HERB POTATOES

Mustard and Herb Potatoes,
Bacon and Cheese-filled Potatoes

4 potatoes, scrubbed
2 teaspoons vegetable oil
30 g/1 oz butter, softened
2 teaspoons chopped fresh parsley
1¹/₂ teaspoons dried mixed herbs
1 teaspoon wholegrain mustard

1   Place potatoes in an ovenproof dish, brush with oil and bake for 1 hour or until tender. Set aside to cool for 2-3 minutes.

2   Place butter, parsley, herbs and mustard in a bowl and mix to combine.

3   Cut a cross in top of each potato and using the thumbs, push the sides of the potato up to force open the cross. Place a spoonful of seasoned butter in each cross and serve immediately.

Serves 4

Oven temperature
200°C, 400°F, Gas 6

The mustard and herb butter on these jacket-baked potatoes is just as tasty served with grilled or barbecued steak.

45

Main Meals in Minutes

Just because you're busy doesn't mean you can't prepare stylish and tasty meals. With these recipes you can have a delicious dinner on the table in no time at all.

Quick 'n' Easy Family Meat Pie

Oven temperature
220°C, 425°F, Gas 7

2 teaspoons vegetable oil
2 onions, chopped
1 clove garlic, crushed
750 g/1¹/₂ lb lean beef mince
155 g/5 oz button mushrooms, sliced
1 tablespoon gravy powder
1 tablespoon flour
2 tablespoons tomato sauce
250 g/8 oz prepared shortcrust pastry
1 egg, separated
250 g/8 oz prepared puff pastry

Milk can be substituted for egg glazing, but a richer browning is obtained with the use of egg glazing for savoury pies.

1   Heat oil in a saucepan over a medium heat, add onions and garlic and cook, stirring, for 3 minutes or until onions are tender. Add beef and cook for 4 minutes longer or until beef is cooked through. Stir mushrooms, gravy powder, flour and tomato sauce into pan and cook, stirring constantly, for 2 minutes or until mixture thickens. Remove pan from heat and allow to cool.

2   Roll out shortcrust pastry on lightly floured surface and cut to fit a greased 23 cm/9 in pie plate. Brush pastry with egg white and spoon filling into pastry case.

3   Roll out puff pastry and cut to make a lid for the pie. Place pastry over filling, trim and pinch edges to seal and reserve trimmings. Brush top of pie with beaten egg yolk and using a sharp knife, make a narrow slit in the centre to allow steam to escape. Decorate pie with reserved trimmings.

4   Bake for 10 minutes, reduce oven temperature to 190°C/375°F/Gas 5 and bake for 15 minutes longer or until pastry is puffed and golden. Serve hot with vegetables or salad.

Serves 6

Quick 'n' Easy Family Meat Pie

FISH CUTLETS WITH LIME SAUCE

1/3 cup/90 mL/3 fl oz chicken stock
1/3 cup/90 mL/3 fl oz dry white wine
4 x 155 g/5 oz white fish cutlets
lime twists
chopped spring onions

LIME SAUCE
1/4 cup/75 g/2 1/2 oz lime marmalade
2 teaspoons cornflour blended with
1 tablespoon water
1 teaspoon sugar

1 Place stock and wine in a large frying pan over a medium heat and bring to the boil. Reduce heat to simmering, gently lower fish into pan, cover and poach for 5 minutes or until fish changes colour and is cooked through. Remove fish from pan, drain and reserve 2/3 cup/170 mL/5 1/2 fl oz liquid. Arrange fish on serving plates and set aside to keep warm.

2 To make sauce, place marmalade, blended cornflour, sugar and reserved liquid in a small saucepan, mix to combine and cook over a medium heat, stirring constantly, for 2 minutes or until sauce boils and thickens slightly. Spoon sauce over fish, garnish with lime twists and spring onions and serve.

Serves 4

Any firm-fleshed fish cutlets or thick boneless fillets may be used in this recipe.

LEMON MUSTARD DRUMSTICKS

2 tablespoons lemon juice
2 tablespoons Italian dressing
1 teaspoon freshly ground
black pepper
1 teaspoon Worcestershire sauce
1/2 teaspoon prepared mustard
500 g/1 lb chicken drumsticks
pinch ground paprika

1 Place lemon juice, dressing, black pepper, Worcestershire sauce and mustard in a small bowl and mix to combine. Brush mixture over chicken and sprinkle with paprika.

2 Place chicken under a preheated medium grill and cook, turning frequently, for 30 minutes, or until golden brown and cooked through, brushing with lemon mixture during cooking.

Serves 2

Serve drumsticks as picnic fare or party nibbles with plenty of paper napkins for sticky fingers!

Fish Cutlets with Lime Sauce

ALMOND CHICKEN

1 tablespoon cornflour
$^1/_4$ teaspoon ground nutmeg
$^1/_4$ teaspoon five spice powder
375 g/12 oz boneless chicken breast
fillets, thinly sliced
2 tablespoons vegetable oil
2 carrots, cut into julienne strips
125 g/4 oz blanched whole almonds
440 g/14 oz canned straw mushrooms,
drained
220 g/7 oz canned pineapple pieces,
drained
4 spring onions, chopped
$^1/_2$ cup/125 mL/4 fl oz coconut milk

1 Place cornflour, nutmeg and five spice powder in a bowl and mix to combine. Add chicken to bowl and stir to coat with cornflour mixture.

2 Heat oil in a frying pan or wok over a medium heat, add chicken, carrots and almonds and stir-fry for 5 minutes or until chicken is just cooked.

3 Add mushrooms, pineapple and spring onions to pan and stir-fry for 5 minutes longer. Stir coconut milk into mixture, bring to the boil, then reduce heat and simmer for 5 minutes or until chicken is tender and cooked through. Serve with boiled rice.

Serves 4

Powdered coconut milk can be made up according to packet instructions if canned is not available.
If straw mushrooms are unavailable use ordinary canned mushrooms instead.

THAI-STYLE SPARE RIBS

1 cup/250 mL/8 fl oz apricot nectar
or purée
$^2/_3$ cup/170 mL/5$^1/_2$ fl oz coconut milk
2 tablespoons brown sugar
2 tablespoons Thai-style seasoning
6 beef spare ribs

1 Place nectar or purée, coconut milk, sugar and seasoning in a large shallow dish and mix to combine. Add spare ribs, toss to coat and marinate, covered, in the refrigerator for 24 hours.

2 Place ribs on a rack in a baking dish and cook, brushing occasionally with marinade, for 30 minutes, turn ribs over and cook for 30 minutes longer or until cooked through and tender.

Serves 6

Oven temperature
200°C, 400°F, Gas 6

If Thai-style seasoning is unavailable, substitute red or green chilli paste and reduce amount used to 1 tablespoon, more or less, to taste, as desired.

PORK WITH ORANGE SAUCE

30 g/1 oz butter
6 pork butterfly steaks
2 tablespoons orange-flavoured
liqueur (optional)
1 orange, sliced

ORANGE SAUCE
1 tablespoon finely grated orange rind
1 tablespoon finely grated fresh ginger
1 clove garlic, crushed
2 tablespoons brown sugar
$^1/_2$ cup/125 mL/4 fl oz orange juice
2 tablespoons vegetable oil
2 teaspoons finely grated lemon rind
freshly ground black pepper

1 Melt butter in large frying pan over medium heat, add pork and cook for 3 minutes on each side or until pork is golden brown.

2 To make sauce, place orange rind, ginger, garlic, sugar, orange juice, oil, lemon rind, and black pepper to taste in a bowl and mix to combine. Pour over pork and simmer, covered, for 20 minutes or until pork is tender and cooked through.

3 Using a slotted spoon, remove pork from pan, arrange on a serving platter and set aside to keep warm. Bring sauce to the boil, stir liqueur, if using, and orange slices into mixture, reduce heat and simmer for 3 minutes. Arrange orange slices across pork and spoon over sauce. Serve immediately.

Serves 6

Serve accompanied with baby potatoes and a steamed green vegetable.

GINGERED CHICKEN

2 tablespoons flour
3 teaspoons ground ginger
2 teaspoons finely grated fresh ginger
1 kg/2 lb boneless chicken breast
fillets, sliced
$^1/_4$ cup/60 mL/2 fl oz vegetable oil
1 onion, sliced
280 g/9 oz canned bamboo shoots,
drained
1 red pepper, sliced
$^2/_3$ cup/170 mL/5$^1/_2$ fl oz chicken
stock
2 tablespoons dry sherry
1 tablespoon light soy sauce
125 g/4 oz button mushrooms, sliced
freshly ground black pepper

1 Place flour, ground ginger and fresh ginger in a large bowl, mix to combine, add chicken and stir to coat chicken with flour mixture.

2 Heat oil in a large wok or frying pan over a medium heat and stir-fry chicken, in batches, until golden brown. Remove chicken from pan and set aside.

3 Add onion to pan and cook, stirring, for 3 minutes or until tender. Stir bamboo shoots, red pepper, stock, sherry and soy sauce into pan, add chicken, bring to the boil, reduce heat and simmer, covered for 5 minutes or until chicken is tender and cooked through.

4 Add mushrooms to mixture and cook for 3 minutes longer. Season to taste with black pepper and serve.

Serves 8

Store fresh mushrooms in a brown paper bag or a calico 'mushroom bag' in the refrigerator. Storing mushrooms in plastic will make them sweat.

GINGERED FISH KEBABS

500 g/1 lb firm white fish fillets
$^1/_4$ cup/60 mL/2 fl oz lemon juice
2 tablespoons sesame seeds, toasted
1 tablespoon Worcestershire sauce
1 teaspoon finely grated fresh ginger
$^1/_2$ teaspoon finely chopped fresh
red chilli
1 clove garlic, crushed
freshly ground black pepper

To prepare kebabs in advance, complete step 1 and thread fish onto skewers, cover and refrigerate for up to 4 hours before cooking.

1 Cut fish into 1 cm/$^1/_2$ in thick strips. Place lemon juice, sesame seeds, Worcestershire sauce, ginger, chilli, garlic and black pepper to taste in a bowl. Add fish and toss to coat.

2 Thread and weave fish onto skewers, reserving marinade. Cook kebabs under a preheated hot grill for 5-6 minutes or until fish is cooked through, turning once and brushing with reserved marinade.

Serves 4

TROUT WITH RAINBOW DRESSING

6 whole trout, cleaned and scaled
$^1/_4$ cup/60 mL/2 fl oz lemon juice
$^1/_4$ teaspoon freshly ground black pepper
1$^1/_2$ cups/375 mL/12 fl oz white wine
1$^1/_2$ cups/375 mL/ 12 fl oz chicken
stock
6 spring onions, chopped

RAINBOW DRESSING
$^3/_4$ cup/185 mL/6 fl oz mayonnaise
$^3/_4$ cup/185 g/6 oz sour cream
freshly ground black pepper
2 teaspoons tomato paste (purée)
$^1/_2$ teaspoon dried basil leaves
6 leaves spinach, blanched
1 tablespoon chopped fresh parsley

To bone trout, cut underside of fish from cavity to tail with tip of a sharp knife open the cavity and gently loosen transverse bones from flesh on both sides. Snip the backbone at tail and head with scissors and carefully peel backbone and transverse bones from fish.
To remove skin before serving, cut skin neatly at head and tail and carefully peel away, taking care not to damage the flesh underneath.

1 Bone trout, remove eyes and place in a shallow dish. Add lemon juice and black pepper and set aside to marinate for 10 minutes. Drain trout and reserve marinade.

2 Place wine, stock, spring onions, and trout in a shallow flameproof baking dish over a medium heat and bring to the boil. Reduce heat and gently poach trout for 10 minutes or until trout changes colour and is cooked through. Remove from heat and allow trout to cool in liquid.

3 Remove trout from pan, drain and remove skin if desired. Place trout on a serving dish, set aside and keep warm.

4 To make dressing, place reserved marinade, mayonnaise, sour cream and black pepper to taste in a bowl and mix to combine. Divide mixture into three portions, reserving one third. Add tomato paste (purée) and basil to second third of mixture and mix well to combine. Place remaining third in a food processor or blender with spinach and parsley and process until smooth. Spoon dressings in a rainbow pattern beside trout and serve.

Trout with Rainbow Dressing

Serves 6

INDONESIAN CHILLI BEEF

200 g/6¹/₂ oz rice vermicelli
1 tablespoon peanut oil
250 g/8 oz rump steak, thinly sliced
1 onion, quartered
1 fresh red chilli, finely chopped
2 cloves garlic, crushed
freshly ground black pepper
¹/₂ cucumber, peeled, seeded and diced
45 g/1¹/₂ oz roasted peanuts

1   Place vermicelli in a bowl, pour over enough hot water to cover and soak for 10 minutes. Drain, set aside and keep warm.

2   Heat oil in a large frying pan or wok over a medium heat, add beef, onion, chilli, garlic and black pepper to taste and stir-fry for 5 minutes, or until beef is cooked through.

3   Arrange vermicelli on serving plates and sprinkle with cucumber. Spoon meat over cucumber, sprinkle with peanuts and serve.

Serves 4

Rice vermicelli (or cellophane noodles) do not require cooking after soaking, as the soaking is sufficient to rehydrate and tenderise.

LEMON PISTACHIO SCHNITZELS

185 g/6 oz cornflakes, crushed
60 g/2 oz shelled pistachio nuts, finely chopped
2 tablespoons chopped fresh parsley
1 tablespoon finely grated lemon rind
6 lean veal schnitzels (escalopes)
³/₄ cup/90 g/3 oz seasoned flour
2 eggs beaten with 2 tablespoons milk
60 g/2 oz butter
¹/₄ cup/60 mL/2 fl oz vegetable oil
thin lemon slices
fresh parsley sprigs

LEMON PISTACHIO SAUCE
60 g/2 oz pistachio nuts
³/₄ cup/185 mL/6 fl oz cream (double)
³/₄ cup/185 g/6 oz sour cream
¹/₃ cup/90 mL/3 fl oz brandy
4 spring onions, chopped
2 tablespoons water
2 teaspoons sugar
2 teaspoons finely grated lemon rind
freshly ground black pepper

1   Place cornflake crumbs, chopped pistachio nuts, parsley and lemon rind in a shallow dish and mix to combine. Dust veal with seasoned flour, dip in egg mixture, then press into crumb mixture to coat both sides.

2   Heat butter and oil in a frying pan over a medium heat, add veal and cook for 4 minutes on each side, or until cooked through and browned. Remove veal from pan, set aside and keep warm.

3   To make sauce, drain off all but 1 tablespoon fat from frying pan, add pistachio nuts and cook over a medium heat, stirring, for 2 minutes. Stir cream, sour cream, brandy, spring onions, water, sugar, lemon rind and black pepper to taste into pan and heat gently without boiling. Drizzle sauce over veal, garnish with lemon slices and parsley sprigs and serve.

Serves 6

To prepare veal in advance, complete as far as step 1, wrap each schnitzel separately in freezer bags and freeze for up to 6 weeks in advance.

Lemon Pistachio Schnitzels

PAN-FRIED FISH WITH TOMATO SAUCE

4 x 155 g/5 oz firm white fish fillets
1/2 cup/60 g/2 oz flour
3 tablespoons grated Parmesan cheese
freshly ground black pepper
30 g/1 oz butter
2 tablespoons vegetable oil

FRESH TOMATO SAUCE
1 cup/250 mL/8 fl oz tomato juice
2 spring onions, chopped
1 tablespoon cornflour blended with
2 tablespoons water
1 teaspoon Dijon mustard
1/3 cup/90 mL/3 fl oz thousand island
dressing

1 Place flour, 2 tablespoons Parmesan cheese and black pepper to taste in a plastic food bag, add fillets and shake bag to coat fish in flour mixture, then shake off excess.

2 To make sauce, place tomato juice, spring onions, blended cornflour and mustard in a saucepan over a medium heat, bring to the boil, stirring, and cook for 2 minutes longer. Stir dressing into sauce. Set aside and keep warm.

3 Heat butter and oil in a frying pan over a medium heat, add fish and cook for 4 minutes each side, or until golden brown and cooked through. Remove fish from pan and drain on absorbent kitchen paper.

4 Arrange fish on a serving platter, drizzle with sauce, sprinkle with remaining Parmesan cheese and serve immediately with steamed vegetables.

Serves 4

This treatment for fish works just as well with thin veal schnitzels (escalopes), if preferred.

PORK CHOPS IN CIDER SAUCE

6 lean pork chops
1/4 cup/30 g/1 oz seasoned flour
1 tablespoon vegetable oil
1 onion, sliced
1 clove garlic, crushed
11/4 cups/315 mL/10 fl oz apple cider
1 teaspoon dried rosemary leaves
100 g/31/2 oz prunes, pitted
2 green apples, peeled, cored and
sliced into rings
2 tablespoons cream (double) or
natural yogurt
freshly ground black pepper
1 tablespoon chopped fresh parsley

1 Toss pork in seasoned flour to coat and shake off excess. Heat oil in a frying pan over a medium heat, add chops and cook for 3 minutes on each side or until golden brown.

2 Add onion and garlic to pan and cook for 2 minutes or until onion is tender. Stir cider and rosemary into pan, bring to the boil, reduce heat and simmer, covered, for 20 minutes.

3 Add prunes and apples to mixture, cover and cook for 10 minutes longer, or until pork is tender and cooked through. Stir cream or yogurt and black pepper to taste into pan, sprinkle with parsley and serve.

Serves 6

Steamed brown rice and vegetables make a delicious accompaniment for this saucy pork dish.

Pork Chops in Cider Sauce

VEAL NORMANDY

6 thin slices shoulder ham
6 veal schnitzels (escalopes),
pounded thinly
1 green apple, thinly sliced
45 g/1^1/$_2$ oz alfalfa sprouts
2 cups/125 g/4 oz breadcrumbs, made
from stale bread
2 tablespoons sesame seeds, toasted
2 teaspoons finely grated lemon rind
1 teaspoon ground ginger
^{1}/$_2$ cup/60 g/2 oz seasoned flour
2 eggs, beaten with 1 tablespoon milk
2 tablespoons vegetable oil
30 g/1 oz butter

Serves 6

1 Lay a slice of ham over each schnitzel (escalope). Place a few apple slices and alfalfa sprouts on one side of each ham slice. Fold in half to enclose filling and secure with wooden toothpicks or cocktail sticks.

2 Combine breadcrumbs, sesame seeds, lemon rind and ginger in a shallow dish. Dust each schnitzel (escalope) with seasoned flour, dip into egg mixture and coat with crumb mixture.

3 Heat oil and butter in a frying pan over a medium heat, add schnitzels (escalopes) and cook for 4 minutes each side or until cooked through. Remove toothpicks or cocktail sticks from parcels and serve.

If preferred, small boneless chicken breast fillets may be used in place of the veal schnitzels. Pound chicken gently between sheets of nonstick baking paper until quite thin before filling and coating.

FISH FILLETS WITH LEMON BUTTER

Microwave

6 x 155 g/5 oz boneless white fish
fillets
1 tablespoon tarragon vinegar
1 tablespoon lemon juice
2 spring onions, chopped
pinch dried tarragon
freshly ground black pepper
lemon twists
fresh parsley sprigs

LEMON BUTTER
125 g/4 oz butter, softened
1 tablespoon finely grated lemon rind
2 teaspoons lemon juice
2 tablespoons chopped fresh parsley

Serves 6

To cook conventionally, place fish fillets, vinegar, lemon juice, spring onions, tarragon and lemon pepper in a frying pan over a medium heat, reduce heat to low, cover and cook for 5 minutes, or until fish flakes when tested with a fork.

1   To make Lemon Butter, place butter, lemon rind, lemon juice and parsley in a bowl and mix well to combine. Using a sheet of nonstick baking paper, shape mixture into a log, 2 cm/^{3}/4 in in diameter. Freeze until firm, cut into twelve slices and set aside.

2   Place fish fillets, vinegar, lemon juice, spring onions, tarragon and black pepper to taste in a shallow microwavable dish, cover and cook on HIGH (100%) for 4 minutes, turn fish and cook for 2 minutes longer. Drain and serve topped with Lemon Butter, a lemon twist and parsley sprig.

VEAL ROLLS WITH APRICOT SAUCE

4 veal schnitzels (escalopes),
pounded thinly
8 slices wholegrain bread, crusts
removed
30 g/1 oz butter
1 tablespoon vegetable oil

SPINACH RICOTTA FILLING
^{1}/2 bunch/250 g/8 oz fresh spinach,
blanched and chopped
45 g/1^1/2 oz chopped pecans, toasted
2 tablespoons ricotta cheese
1 tablespoon lemon juice
1 tablespoon orange juice
^{1}/4 teaspoon dried basil
^{1}/4 teaspoon dried thyme

APRICOT SAUCE
200 g/6^1/2 oz canned, unsweetened
apricots, drained
200 g/6^1/2 oz low-fat natural yogurt
freshly ground black pepper

To blanch spinach, wash, drain and place spinach in a saucepan with just the water clinging to its leaves and cook, covered, over a medium heat shaking pan occasionally until just wilted. Drain well and press spinach between two plates to remove excess water.

2   To make filling, combine spinach, pecans, ricotta cheese, lemon juice, orange juice, basil and thyme. Spoon mixture evenly over bread-topped schnitzels (escalopes) and roll up firmly. Secure with wooden toothpicks or cocktail sticks and cut each roll in half.

3   Heat butter and oil in a frying pan over a medium heat and cook rolls, turning frequently, for 10 minutes, or until cooked through. Remove from pan and set aside to keep warm. Remove toothpicks or cocktail sticks.

4   To make sauce, reserve one-third of apricots. Place remaining apricots in a food processor or blender and process until smooth. Place apricot purée in a saucepan over a medium heat, add yogurt and black pepper to taste and cook over a low heat, stirring, for 1-2 minutes or until heated. Slice veal and serve with sauce and reserved apricots.

Veal Rolls with Apricot Sauce

1   Cover each schnitzel (escalope) with 2 slices of bread.

Serves 4

CURRIED SEAFOOD ROULADE

Oven temperature
200°C, 400°F, Gas 6

315 g/10 oz mixed seafood, such as
prawns, scallops and fish fillets
1 1/2 cups/375 mL/12 fl oz white wine
1 carrot, cut into thin strips
1 zucchini (courgette), cut into
thin strips
60 g/2 oz butter
6 spring onions, chopped
1 teaspoon curry powder
1/4 cup/30 g/1 oz flour
1/2 cup/125 mL/4 fl oz coconut milk
1/4 cup/60 mL/2 fl oz milk

TOMATO ROULADE
60 g/2 oz butter
1/2 cup/60 g/2 oz flour
1 cup/250 mL/8 fl oz milk
2 tablespoons tomato paste (purée)
1 tablespoon wholegrain mustard
4 eggs, separated

1 Prepare seafood and cut into
1 cm/1/2 in pieces. Place prepared
seafood, wine, carrot and zucchini
(courgette) in a saucepan over a
medium heat, bring to simmering and
cook for 3 minutes or until seafood is
just cooked. Drain seafood mixture,
reserving 1/4 cup/60 mL/2 fl oz of liquid
and set aside.

2 Melt butter in the same pan over a
medium heat, add spring onions and
curry powder and cook, stirring, for
1 minute. Add flour to pan and cook,
stirring, for 1 minute. Remove pan from
heat and gradually whisk in coconut
milk, milk and reserved cooking liquid.
Return pan to heat and cook, stirring
constantly, for 4-5 minutes or until
sauce boils and thickens. Remove pan
from heat, add seafood mixture and
mix gently to combine. Set aside to
cool.

3 To make roulade, melt butter in a
separate saucepan over a medium heat,
add flour and cook, stirring, for
1 minute. Remove pan from heat and
gradually whisk in milk. Return pan to
heat and cook, stirring constantly, for
4-5 minutes or until sauce boils and
thickens. Remove pan from heat and
stir in tomato paste (purée), mustard
and egg yolks and mix until ingredients
are blended and mixture is smooth.

4 Place egg whites into a clean bowl
and beat until stiff peaks form. Fold egg
whites into roulade mixture. Spoon
into a greased and lined 26 x 32 cm/
10 1/2 x 12 3/4 in Swiss roll tin and cook
for 10-15 minutes or until firm. Turn
roulade onto a clean teatowel, carefully
remove lining paper and roll up in the
towel from the short end. Set aside to
cool slightly.

5 Unroll roulade and spread with
seafood filling, leaving a 1 cm/1/2 in
border. Reroll roulade and serve sliced.

Serves 6

For the seafood filling, use a
mixture of firm white fish
fillets, scallops and peeled
and deveined uncooked
prawns.

Chicken with Mango Salsa

CHICKEN WITH MANGO SALSA

¹/4 cup/60 mL/2 fl oz white wine
2 tablespoons peanut oil
1 tablespoon lemon juice
1 clove garlic, crushed
¹/4 teaspoon finely grated fresh ginger
freshly ground black pepper
4 boneless chicken breast fillets

MANGO SALSA
15 g/¹/2 oz butter
2 spring onions, chopped
1 tomato, peeled and chopped
1 teaspoon chilli sauce
1 mango, peeled and chopped

Serves 4

1 Combine wine, oil, lemon juice, garlic, ginger and black pepper to taste. Add chicken and marinate overnight.

2 To make salsa, melt butter in a saucepan over a medium heat, add spring onions and tomato and cook until onions are tender. Stir in chilli sauce and mango and cook 5 minutes. Cool, then chill.

3 Drain chicken and grill for 5 minutes on each side or until cooked. Serve with salsa.

For a fajita-style meal, cut chicken into thin shreds after cooking and serve with pan-fried onions, shredded lettuce and mango salsa in warmed flour tortillas.

CHICKEN PARCELS HOLLANDAISE
Microwave

4 large lettuce leaves
4 boneless chicken breast fillets,
pounded thinly
100 g/3 $^1/_2$ oz smoked salmon or
smoked trout
1 avocado, each half sliced into sixths
1 large orange, segmented

ORANGE HOLLANDAISE
60 g/2 oz butter
$^1/_2$ teaspoon Dijon mustard
2 egg yolks
$^1/_4$ cup/60 mL/2 fl oz cream (double)
1 teaspoon finely grated orange rind
$^1/_2$ teaspoon lemon juice

1   Place lettuce leaves onto a microwavable dish, cover and cook on HIGH (100%) for 1 minute. Plunge lettuce into cold water, pat dry and set aside.

2   Place chicken in a microwavable dish, cover and cook on HIGH (100%) for 3-5 minutes or until almost cooked. Drain chicken. Place each fillet on a lettuce leaf, top with a slice of salmon and some avocado and orange. Fold lettuce leaves around chicken, tucking in edges, to form parcels. Secure with wooden toothpicks or cocktail sticks.

3   Place chicken parcels into a greased, shallow microwavable dish, cover and cook on HIGH (100%) for 3 minutes. Set aside and keep warm.

4   To make hollandaise, place butter into a large microwavable jug and cook on HIGH (100%) for 30 seconds. Add mustard, egg yolks, cream, orange rind and lemon juice and whisk until well blended. Return jug to oven and cook for 1-1 $^1/_2$ minutes longer, pausing to stir every 15 seconds. Whisk until smooth and light.

5   Remove toothpicks or cocktail sticks from chicken parcels. Serve with hollandaise and garnish with remaining avocado and orange.

Serves 4

Parcels may be prepared in advance to the end of step 2. Place parcels in a greased shallow dish, cover and chill for up to 3 hours before cooking. Stand hollandaise, covered, at room temperature or chill, until ready to use. To serve parcels, proceed from step 3 and add 1 minute to cooking time. Reheat hollandaise for 20 seconds, whisk and serve.

Chicken Parcels Hollandaise

FILLET MIGNON WITH MUSTARD SAUCE

4 rashers bacon
4 thick pieces beef fillet steak
30 g/1 oz butter

MUSTARD SAUCE
4 spring onions, sliced
1/2 cup/125 mL/4 fl oz port
1/2 cup/125 mL/4 fl oz beef stock
freshly ground black pepper
2 tablespoons Dijon mustard
2 tablespoons cream (double)

Accompany steaks with a hearty Caesar salad and crusty bread or a favourite selection of steamed green and yellow vegetables.

1 Wrap a rasher of bacon around each steak and secure with string. Melt butter in a frying pan over a medium heat, add steaks and cook for 3 minutes on each side or until cooked to your liking. Remove steaks from pan, set aside and keep warm.

2 To make sauce, add spring onions to same pan and cook, stirring, for 2 minutes or until spring onions are tender. Stir port, stock and black pepper to taste into pan, bring to the boil, reduce heat and simmer for 3-5 minutes or until liquid reduces by half. Stir in mustard and cream and cook, stirring, for 2-3 minutes or until sauce is heated. Spoon over steaks and serve.

Serves 4

FILLETS WITH MUSHROOM SAUCE

8 slices bread, suitable for toasting
8 thick pieces beef fillet steak
freshly ground black pepper
90 g/3 oz butter
1 avocado, sliced into eighths
1 tablespoon French dressing

MUSHROOM SAUCE
1 onion, chopped
1 clove garlic, chopped
250 g/8 oz button mushrooms, sliced
2 tablespoons flour
1/2 teaspoon paprika
1/2 cup/125 mL/4 fl oz beef stock
1/3 cup/90 mL/3 fl oz red wine
2 tablespoons tomato purée
1 tablespoon brandy
1 teaspoon French mustard
1/2 cup/125 mL/4 fl oz cream (double)

Use fresh asparagus, when available, instead of canned. Cook fresh asparagus spears in the microwave oven, allowing 2-3 spears per person.

1 Cut bread into 10 cm/4 in rounds and toast until golden brown.

2 Season steaks with black pepper and tie into neat shapes, if necessary, with kitchen string. Melt butter in a frying pan over a medium heat, add steaks and cook on both sides to desired doneness. Remove steaks from pan and set aside to keep warm.

3 To make sauce, return pan to a medium heat, add onion, garlic and mushrooms and cook, stirring, for 3 minutes. Add flour and paprika and cook, stirring, for 1 minute. Remove pan from heat and gradually whisk in stock, wine, tomato purée, brandy and mustard. Return pan to heat and cook, stirring constantly, until sauce boils and thickens. Reduce heat and simmer for 5 minutes longer. Remove pan from heat and stir in cream.

4 To serve, toss avocado with dressing to coat. Place each steak on a toasted croûton, remove string, drizzle with sauce and garnish with avocado.

Serves 8

Fillet Mignon with Mustard Sauce

64

DESSERTS WITH DASH

No time to prepare a dessert? You have with these recipes and you don't have to have a sweet tooth to enjoy them – they're simply irresistible.

STRAWBERRIES AND ORANGES IN PORT

375 g/12 oz strawberries, halved
2 oranges, peeled and sliced crosswise
$^1/_4$ cup/60 mL/2 fl oz port
1$^1/_4$ cups/315 mL/10 fl oz cream
(double)
1 tablespoon icing sugar, sifted
1 teaspoon vanilla essence

1 Place strawberries and oranges in a bowl. Sprinkle with port and toss to combine. Cover and set aside to macerate for 30-60 minutes.

2 Place cream, icing sugar and vanilla essence in a bowl and beat until soft peaks form.

3 Divide fruit mixture between four serving dishes and top with cream.

Serves 4

Other liqueurs such as amaretto, Curaçao or Grand Marnier or a flavoured brandy may be used in place of the port, if preferred.

Strawberries and Oranges in Port

PEARS WITH KIWIFRUIT SAUCE

Microwave

2 cups/500 mL/16 fl oz water
1 cup/250 g/8 oz sugar
5 cm/2 in strip lemon rind
2 cinnamon sticks
1 whole clove
2-3 drops red food colouring
6 pears, peeled, halved and cored

KIWIFRUIT SAUCE
6 kiwifruit, peeled and quartered
1 tablespoon green ginger wine

1 Place water, sugar, lemon rind, cinnamon, clove and food colouring in a large microwavable jug and cook on HIGH (100%) for 5 minutes, stirring after 2^1/$_2$ minutes, or until sugar dissolves and a syrup forms.

2 Place pears in a microwavable dish, pour syrup over pears, cover and cook for 4-5 minutes longer, or until pears are just tender. Set aside to cool in syrup.

3 To make sauce, remove seeds from kiwifruit. Place kiwifruit flesh in a food processor or blender and process until smooth. Stir in wine.

4 Using a sharp knife, slice pear halves from base to within 2 cm/^{3}/$_4$ in of stem. Open each pear into a fan and place onto serving plates. Serve with Kiwifruit Sauce.

Serves 6

For an attractive finish, remove cores from pears with a melon baller. Seeds should be removed from kiwifruit as they make the sauce bitter when processed in a food processor or blender.

PEANUT PRALINE ICE CREAM

Microwave

1 cup/250 g/8 oz raw (muscovado) or demerara sugar
^{1}/$_2$ cup/125 mL/4 fl oz water
60 g/2 oz chopped peanuts, crushed
^{1}/$_4$ cup/60 g/2 oz smooth peanut butter
^{1}/$_4$ cup/90 g/3 oz honey
2 litres/3^1/$_2$ pt vanilla ice cream, softened

1 Place sugar and water in a large microwavable jug and cook, stirring twice, on HIGH (100%) for 2 minutes or until sugar dissolves. Cook, without stirring, for 10-11 minutes longer or until syrup is golden. Stir in nuts.

2 Pour toffee mixture onto an oiled baking tray, allow to set, then break toffee into pieces. Place toffee into a food processor or blender and process until roughly crushed.

3 Place peanut butter and honey in a microwavable dish and cook on HIGH (100%) for 30 seconds. Stir in crushed toffee, then fold mixture into ice cream. Return ice cream to container and freeze until firm.

Serves 8

Chocolate or coffee-flavoured ice cream is also delicious when flavoured with crunchy peanut praline.

Bananas in Coconut Cream

BANANAS IN COCONUT CREAM

90 g/3 oz sultanas
45 g/1$^1/_2$ oz shredded coconut
1 cup/250 mL/8 fl oz coconut milk
15 g/$^1/_2$ oz butter
4 firm bananas, sliced
2 tablespoons palm or brown sugar

1   Place sultanas, coconut and coconut milk in a bowl and mix to combine. Set aside to soak for 10 minutes.

2   Melt butter in a frying pan over a medium heat. Add bananas and cook, stirring, for 4-5 minutes or until bananas are golden. Remove bananas from pan and set aside.

3   Add coconut milk mixture and sugar to pan and stirring constantly bring to the boil. Return bananas to pan, toss to combine and serve immediately.

Serves

Palm sugar is available from Oriental food stores and some supermarkets. It is a coarse brown sugar that is made from the sap of the Palmyra palm. It is used extensively in the cooking of India and Southeast Asia.

BRANDIED PEACH PARFAIT

4 fresh peaches, peeled
brown sugar
1¼ cups/315 mL/10 fl oz cream
(double), whipped
brandy

1 Slice peaches thinly and reserve a few slices for garnishing. Divide remaining peach slices between four dessert dishes. Sprinkle with sugar, then top with a thick layer of cream and drizzle with brandy to taste.

2 Cover dishes with plastic food wrap and refrigerate for at least 6 hours to allow the different flavours to mingle. Just prior to serving, decorate with reserved peach slices.

Serves 4

This dessert can be made a day ahead of serving and chilled in the refrigerator overnight. Strawberries may be substituted for peaches.

SCARLET FRUITS WITH CHANTILLY CREAM

¼ cup/60 g/2 oz raw (muscovado) or
demerera sugar
½ cup/125 mL/4 fl oz water
1 tablespoon orange-flavoured liqueur
2 teaspoons grenadine syrup or
raspberry cordial
6 red plums, cut into eighths
375 g/12 oz strawberries
315 g/10 oz raspberries or
250 g/8 oz frozen raspberries
¼ small watermelon, cut into balls

SOUR CHANTILLY CREAM
1¼ cups/315 g/10 oz sour cream
2 tablespoons icing sugar, sifted
1 teaspoon vanilla essence

1 Place raw (muscovado) or demerera sugar and water in a saucepan and heat over a medium heat, stirring, until sugar dissolves. Stir in liqueur and grenadine or cordial. Remove pan from heat and chill.

2 Place plums, strawberries, raspberries and watermelon in a bowl and toss to combine. Pour syrup over fruit and chill for 2-3 hours.

3 To make cream, place sour cream, icing sugar and vanilla essence in a bowl and mix to combine. Serve with fruit.

Serves 6

Grenadine syrup is red in colour and was originally made from pomegranates. It is mainly used as a colouring in cocktails and is available from liquor outlets and some supermarkets.

Scarlet Fruits with Chantilly Cream

RUM AND RAISIN CHEESECAKE

100 g/3¹/₂ oz dark chocolate, melted
1 tablespoon vegetable oil

RUM AND RAISIN FILLING
3 teaspoons gelatine
1 tablespoon hot water
250 g/8 oz cream cheese, softened
2 tablespoons sugar
1 teaspoon vanilla essence
¹/₄ cup/60 mL/2 fl oz dark rum
185 g/6 oz raisins, chopped
1¹/₄ cups/315 mL/10 fl oz cream
(double), lightly whipped
chocolate caraque

To make chocolate caraque, pour melted chocolate over a cool work surface such as marble, ceramic or granite. Spread it out to form a thin even layer and allow to set at room temperature. Holding a long sharp knife at a 45° angle, pull gently over the surface of the chocolate to from scrolls.

1 Place chocolate and oil in a heatproof bowl set over a saucepan of simmering water and cook, stirring occasionally, until mixture is smooth. Remove bowl from pan and set aside to cool slightly.

2 Spread chocolate mixture evenly over base and 4 cm/1¹/₂ in up sides of a lightly greased and foil-lined 20 cm/8 in springform tin. Refrigerate for 5 minutes or until set.

3 To make filling, dissolve gelatine in hot water. Set aside to cool. Place cream cheese and sugar in a bowl and beat until soft. Add gelatine mixture, vanilla essence, rum and raisins to mixture and mix to combine. Fold cream into cream cheese mixture and pour into chocolate shell. Refrigerate for 2-3 hours or until filling is set.

4 Just prior to serving, remove cheesecake from tin and decorate with chocolate caraque.

Serves 8-10

VANILLA CREAM FUDGE

3 cups/750 g/1¹/₂ lb raw (muscovado)
or demerera sugar
1¹/₄ cups/315 mL/10 fl oz cream
(double)
1 cup/250 mL/8 fl oz milk
90 g/3 oz butter
¹/₄ teaspoon cream of tartar
2 tablespoons liquid glucose
2 teaspoons vanilla essence

Fudge can be made ahead of time and stored in an airtight container in the refrigerator.

1 Place sugar, cream, milk, butter, cream of tartar and glucose in a saucepan, cook over a medium heat, stirring constantly, for 4-5 minutes or until sugar dissolves.

2 Bring mixture to the boil and boil until it reaches the soft ball stage (116°C/240°F) on a sugar thermometer. Remove pan from heat and set aside to cool for 5 minutes.

3 Stir vanilla essence into mixture and beat for 3-5 minutes or until it is thick and creamy. Pour mixture into a lined 26 x 32 cm/10¹/₂ x 12³/₄ in Swiss roll tin and allow to set at room temperature. Cut into squares.

Makes 48 squares

Rum and Raisin Cheesecake

MELON FREEZE

2¹/₄ teaspoons gelatine
2 tablespoons hot water
1 large rockmelon (cantaloupe),
seeded and diced
2¹/₃ cups/600 mL/1 pt buttermilk
¹/₂ cup/30 g/1 oz skim milk powder
1 teaspoon liquid sweetener

1   Dissolve gelatine in hot water and set aside to cool.

2   Place rockmelon (cantaloupe) and buttermilk in a food processor or blender and process until smooth.

3   Stir gelatine mixture into buttermilk mixture. Pour into freezer trays and freeze for 30 minutes or mixture starts to form crystals around the edges.

4   Place mixture in a bowl, add milk powder and sweetener and beat until thick and foamy. Return mixture to freezer tray and freeze for 2-3 hours or mixture until is firm. To serve, use a fork to flake frozen mixture into chilled serving dishes.

Serves 6

A sweetened fresh raspberry or strawberry purée looks pretty spooned over this low kilojoule (calorie), low-fat and no-sugar sorbet.

SOUFFLE ORANGES

Oven temperature
200°C, 400°F, Gas 6

2 oranges, halved
60 g/2 oz butter
2 tablespoons flour
2 tablespoons sugar
1 cup/250 mL/8 fl oz milk
2 teaspoons orange juice
2 eggs, separated
icing sugar, sifted

1   Remove flesh from orange halves to make four thin shells, take care not to tear the skins of the oranges. Set shells aside.

2   Melt butter in a saucepan over a medium heat, add flour and cook, stirring, for 1 minute. Remove pan from heat and gradually whisk in sugar, milk and orange juice. Return pan to heat and cook, stirring constantly, until mixture boils and thickens. Remove pan from heat and set aside to cool slightly.

3   Beat egg yolks into sauce. Place egg whites in a bowl and beat until soft peaks form. Fold egg whites into sauce.

4   Divide mixture evenly between orange shells and bake for 20 minutes or until soufflés are puffed and golden. Dust with icing sugar and serve immediately.

Serves 4

Soufflé oranges may be refrigerated for up to 24 hours before baking, if desired.

PEACHES ROMANOFF

4 peaches, peeled and sliced
^{1}/$_2$ cup/125 mL/4 fl oz orange juice
^{1}/$_3$ cup/90 mL/3 fl oz orange-flavoured liqueur
2 tablespoons icing sugar

1   Place peaches, orange juice, liqueur and icing sugar in a bowl and toss to combine. Cover and chill for 1 hour.

2   Divide peaches and syrup between four serving dishes. Serve chilled or at room temperature.

Serves 4

For an extra touch of luxury accompany this dessert with lightly whipped cream. Substitute canned peach halves or fresh strawberries if fresh peaches are unavailable.

Soufflé Oranges

CHOCOLATE JAFFA BALLS

125 g/4 oz cream cheese, softened
1 teaspoon finely grated orange rind
2 tablespoons orange juice
2 cups/125 g/4 oz chocolate cake
crumbs
90 g/3 oz coconut, toasted
2 tablespoons finely chopped glacé
ginger

To make cake crumbs, make and bake a chocolate packet cake mix according to directions. Place cake in a food processor or blender and process into crumbs. Store crumbs in the freezer until required.

1 Place cream cheese, orange rind and orange juice in a bowl and beat until smooth. Fold cake crumbs, 45 g/1^1/$_2$ oz coconut and ginger into cream cheese mixture. Cover and chill until mixture is firm enough to roll into balls.

2 Roll teaspooons of mixture into small balls. Toss balls in remaining coconut, place on a plate lined with plastic food wrap and chill.

Makes 36

MILKY FRUIT AND NUT SWEETMEATS

125 g/4 oz white chocolate
1 tablespoon vegetable oil
90 g/3 oz chopped mixed glacé fruit,
such as cherries, ginger, pineapple and
apricots
60 g/2 oz pecans, toasted and chopped
^{1}/$_4$ cup/60 mL/2 fl oz condensed milk
1 tablespoon orange-flavoured liqueur
125 g/4 oz pecans, toasted and
coarsely ground

Sweetmeats store well for up to 2 weeks in the refrigerator. For longer storage, pack into rigid containers, seal, label, date and store in the freezer.

1 Place chocolate and oil in a heatproof bowl set over a saucepan of simmering water and cook, stirring occasionally, until mixture is smooth. Remove bowl from pan and set aside to cool slightly.

2 Stir glacé fruit, chopped pecans, condensed milk and liqueur into chocolate and mix well to combine. Divide mixture into two portions and shape each into a log. Roll each log in ground pecans to coat, place on a plate lined with plastic food wrap and chill for 2-3 hours before cutting into 5 mm/ ^{1}/$_4$ in thick slices.

Makes approximately 40

*Chocolate Jaffa Balls,
Milky Fruit and Nut Sweetmeats*

SPICY FRUIT COMPOTE

Microwave

155 g/5 oz dried apricots
125 g/4 oz raisins
$^1/_2$ cup/125 mL/4 fl oz water
$^1/_4$ cup/60 mL/2 fl oz Marsala or sweet
sherry
$^1/_4$ teaspoon ground mixed spice
3 green apples, cored, peeled
and chopped
3 firm pears, cored, peeled and
chopped
1 cup/250 mL/8 fl oz apple juice
2 tablespoons brown sugar
60 g/2 oz walnut halves

ORANGE CREME FRAICHE
2 cups/500 mL/16 fl oz cream
(double)
$^1/_2$ cup/125 mL/4 fl oz buttermilk or
yogurt
2 teaspoons finely grated orange rind
2 tablespoons icing sugar, sifted

Spicy Fruit Compote can be made up to 5 days in advance. If you do not have time to make crème fraîche serve the compote with a commercially available crème fraîche or natural yogurt.

1 To make crème fraîche, place cream, buttermilk or yogurt and orange rind in a microwavable bowl and cook on MEDIUM (50%) for 30 seconds or until lukewarm. Cover and set aside to stand at room temperature for 12-24 hours or until thickened. Add icing sugar and mix to combine.

2 Place apricots, raisins, water, Marsala or sherry and mixed spice in a microwavable dish. Cover and cook on HIGH (100%) for 1 minute.

3 Place apples, pears and $^1/_2$ cup/ 125 mL/4 fl oz apple juice into a separate microwavable dish. Cover and cook on HIGH (100%) for 4 minutes. Stir and cook for 4 minutes longer. Stir brown sugar, dried fruit mixture and remaining apple juice into fresh fruit mixture. Cover and cook for 4 minutes. Set aside to stand for 2 minutes.

4 To serve, decorate fruit compote with walnuts and accompany with crème fraîche.

Serves 4

CINNAMON ORANGES

4 oranges, segmented
$^1/_4$ cup/60 g/2 oz sugar
$^1/_4$ teaspoon ground cinnamon

Place orange segments in a bowl, sprinkle with cinnamon and sugar, cover and chill for 1 hour.

Serves 4

To 'dress up' cinnamon oranges for a dinner party, sprinkle 2 tablespoons of orange-flavoured liqueur over orange segments prior to chilling. Delicious served with whipped cream or natural yogurt.

BAKED APPLES WITH APRICOT SAUCE

Microwave

60 g/2 oz raisins, chopped
15 g/$^1/_2$ oz butter, softened
1 tablespoon rum
2 Granny Smith apples, cored
$^2/_3$ cup/170 mL/5$^1/_2$ fl oz apple juice

APRICOT SAUCE
2 tablespoons apricot jam
1 teaspoon arrowroot or cornflour
2 teaspoons water

1   Place raisins, butter and rum in bowl and mix to combine. Fill centre of apples with raisin mixture and place apples in a deep microwavable dish. Drizzle apples with apple juice, cover and cook on HIGH (100%) for 4 minutes or until apples are tender. Remove apples from dish and place on serving plates. Pour any juices into a microwavable jug.

2   To make sauce, stir apricot jam, arrowroot or cornflour and water into juices in jug and cook on HIGH (100%) for 1 minute, stir and cook for 1 minute longer or until sauce boils and thickens. Serve with apples.

Serves 2

When Granny Smiths are unavailable, choose any favourite tart cooking apple that holds its shape well after cooking. Delicious served with cream or ice cream.

STRAWBERRY SUZETTE

500 g/1 lb strawberries

SUZETTE SAUCE
60 g/2 oz butter
$^1/_2$ cup/75 g/2$^1/_2$ oz icing sugar, sifted
$^1/_2$ teaspoon finely grated orange rind
1 cup/250 mL/8 fl oz orange juice
$^1/_4$ cup/60 mL/2 fl oz orange-flavoured liqueur

1   To make sauce, melt butter in a saucepan over a medium heat, add icing sugar, orange rind and orange juice and cook, stirring, for 2 minutes or until mixture comes to the boil. Remove pan from heat and stir in liqueur.

2   Divide strawberries between serving dishes and spoon over hot sauce. Serve immediately.

Serves 6

Serve this easy dessert with a scoop of ice cream or whipped cream and brandy snaps or other dessert biscuits.

CONVENTIONAL ELECTRIC OVEN TEMPERATURE GUIDE

Celsius Settings	Fahrenheit Settings	Foods Suitable
120	250	Meringues, pavlova
140	275	Baked custard
150	300	Rich fruit cake (20 cm/8 in)
160	325	Light fruit cake, shortbread
180	350	Casseroles
		Deep butter cakes
190	375	Shallow butter cakes, meats and fish
200	400	Sponges, biscuits, meat loaf
220	425	Swiss roll, patty cakes, rock cakes
230	450	Shortcrust pastry
240	475	Scones
250	500	Puff pastry

FAN-FORCED ELECTRIC OVEN TEMPERATURE

Celsius Settings	Foods Suitable
100	Meringues, pavlova
120	Baked custard
130	Rich fruit cake (20 cm/8 in)
140	Light fruit cake, shortbread
160	Deep butter cakes, casseroles
170	Shallow butter cakes, meats and fish
180	Sponges, biscuits, meat loaf
200	Swiss roll, patty cakes, rock cakes
210	Shortcrust pastry
240	Puff pastry

POSITIONS OF FOOD IN OVEN

Generally the second shelf from the bottom is recommended if only one item of food is to be cooked. However, two or more items which have a common baking temperature may be cooked using multiple shelf positions. For example, four trays of biscuits can be placed on four separate shelves, or the oven loading may consist of a 23 cm/9 in apple pie, shallow butter cake and a chicken. Remove each item of food as it is cooked. With multiple-shelf baking a little more cooking time could be required, so test food for doneness before removing.

FAN-ASSISTED OVENS

Fan-assisted ovens are designed to give even heat throughout. As temperatures for cooking foods in this type of oven are generally 15-20°C lower than those required by a conventional oven, there is a saving of energy. Preheating the oven is not essential, but better results are obtained if the oven is preheated to the required temperature and the oven thermostat light cuts out.

MICROWAVE OVENS

All microwave recipes were tested using a 600-650 watt microwave oven, times given are a guide only. Foods should be checked before the recommended cooking time is reached as variations in size, thickness and ambient temperature can alter cooking times. It is better to undercook, check, then give extra time if necessary.

APPROXIMATE COOKING TIMES FOR ROASTING MEAT

Type of Meat	Cuts of Meat	Time Per kg/2 lb	Oven Temp	Meat Thermometer Temperatures
BEEF	Standing Rib Rolled Sirloin Rolled Rib Uncorned Silverside Bolar Blade Corner Topside	40 minutes Rare 50 minutes Medium 60 minutes Well Done	180°C (350°F/Gas 4)	60°C (140°F) Rare 70°C (160°F) Medium 75°C (170°F) Well Done
	Fillet Scotch Fillet	40-45 minutes Medium	200°C (400°F/Gas 6)	
VEAL	Shoulder or Leg (with bone in or boned and rolled)	40-50 minutes	180°C (350°F/Gas 4)	75°C (170°F) Well Done
LAMB	Leg, Shoulder, Loin, Rolled Shoulder	40-50 minutes	180°C (350°F/Gas 4)	75°C (170°F) Medium
PORK	Leg Loin	90 minutes	190°C (375°F/Gas 5)	85°C (185°F) Very Well Done

APPROXIMATE COOKING TIMES FOR ROASTING POULTRY

Type of Poultry	Total Cooking Time	Oven Temperature	No. of Serves
Chicken 1-1.4 kg (2-3 lb) 1.5- 2 kg (3-4 lb)	1 hour 1$\frac{1}{2}$-1$\frac{3}{4}$ hours	For all sizes 180°C-190°C (350°F-375°F/ Gas 4-5) until cooked	2-4 4-6
Duck 1.4 kg-1.6 kg (3-3$\frac{1}{2}$ lb) 1.7 kg-2 kg (3$\frac{1}{2}$-4 lb)	1$\frac{1}{2}$-2 hours 2-2$\frac{1}{2}$ hours	For all sizes use 180°C-190°C (350°F-375°F/ Gas 4-5) until cooked	2-3 3-5
Turkey 2.5 kg-4 kg (5-8 lb) 4 kg-6 kg (8-12 lb) 6 kg-8 kg (12-16 lb) 8 kg-10 kg (16-20 lb)	2$\frac{1}{2}$ hours 2$\frac{1}{2}$-2$\frac{3}{4}$ hours 2$\frac{3}{4}$-3 hours 3-3$\frac{1}{2}$ hours	For all sizes 200°C (400°F/Gas 6) for 15 minutes then reset to 180°C (350°F/Gas 4) until cooked	6-10 10-12 16 20-22

INDEX